SET FREE!

SET FREE!

Recognising and Healing
Sexual Sin

JOHN WHITE

eagle
Guildford, Surrey

British Library Cataloguing in Publication Data. A
catalogue record for this book is available from the
British Library.

Published by Eagle, an imprint of Inter Publishing Service
(IPS) Ltd, St Nicholas House, 14 The Mount, Guildford,
Surrey GU2 5HN.

Typeset by Palimpsest Book Production Limited,
Polmont, Stirlingshire

Printed and bound in Great Britain by
Caledonian International Book Manufacturing Ltd, Glasgow

ISBN No: 0 86347 193 5

Contents

Prologue

This book is an abridged version of *Eros Redeemed* which I wrote some years ago, itself an attempt to mark changes in my thinking, in society and among Christians in their attitude to sex and sexual sin, since my first book on the subject, *Eros Defiled*, some twenty years previously.

Set Free! is a shorter, more popular book. I have omitted many personal examples, statistics and some of the more detailed examination of the more extreme ways which Satan uses to distort human sexuality. Whilst briefly attempting to show the strategy of Satan, and of the ancient so-called gods, in relation to sexual sin, my objective, whilst noting the consequences of this sin, is to display God's principles of redemption from any and every type of sexual sin. To be changed we need to get back to Scripture as our prime source of information. *Set Free!* focuses on the means through which God comes to our rescue – whatever the issue. To do so, whilst I have had to cut out a great deal, I have kept almost all the teaching on God's healing and sanctification, i.e. a return toward wholeness and toward the restoration of the damaged image of God in men and women. This book also provides reliable information and statistics in order to make it more approachable, more readable and more practical.

In thinking and writing about these issues, I have also come to the conclusion that while technical problems of one sort or another surround all types of sin, most sexual sins can and should be handled by churches.

Certain knowledge and experience will be needed to help individuals out of this stranglehold. Churches can have and can use that knowledge, and they should play a vastly more important role in the restoration of sexual sinners than they do at present. God is revealing to the church in these days a more profound understanding of sexual sin and how it should be dealt with than he has ever revealed to the human sciences.

My hope is that *Set Free!* shows both churches and individuals how.

Chapter 1

A Sin-Stained Church in a Sex-Sated Society

We are half-hearted creatures, fooling about with drink and sex and ambition when infinite joy is offered us . . . We are far too easily pleased.
C.S. LEWIS

The modern talk about sex being free like any other sense, about the body being beautiful like any tree or flower, is either a description of the Garden of Eden or a piece of thoroughly bad psychology, of which the world grew weary two thousand years ago.
MALCOLM MUGGERIDGE

Years ago I wrote a book on sexual amorality. Many changes affecting our sexual lives have taken place since I wrote *Eros Defiled*. The world has changed. It is a very different one from the world in which I then wrote. There have also been changes in the church, a sliding downhill in sexual standards. And I have changed too. I am not the same person as when I wrote my first book. Let me begin, then, by commenting successively on changes in the world, in the church and in myself.

Changes in the World

Knowledge of every kind has increased exponentially. Philosophies have changed. The Western world and all the cities around the globe are influenced by the changes and are openly sex-crazed. Public and private morality have both changed profoundly.

Feminism, gay liberation and now a growing men's movement have advanced in influence and power. The commercial interests behind pornographic literature and videos are in superb financial health, in spite of many efforts opposing pornography. Public standards of morality slide rapidly downhill toward a precipice. Legislative changes are creating a world around us that is more hostile to Christianity's view of sexuality. As I write, the battle over the rights of women vs. the rights of the unborn is still at its height. Sex crimes increase – and the increase is real, not merely a fabrication of news and publicity. AIDS is with us. Initial optimism about the disease eroded rapidly.

Legislation struggles ineffectively to adapt to the changed sexual standards; problems multiply far more quickly than legislated answers. New inheritance problems spring into existence with the acceptance of 'test-tube' babies. International organizations and civil forces of law and order cannot cope adequately with complaints related to prostitution and other sex crimes.

Rape increases. The increase seems to be real, not merely the result of recent trends for women to report rapes to the police. Violent sex crimes are so common that as news items we ignore them – but we start looking over our shoulders on dark nights.

Hard-core porn and even kiddie porn are with us. Adult-child sex has become *de rigueur* in certain circles. Acts of brutality are enacted on video-tapes, commonly acts against women – all designed to inflame the watcher with perverse passion.

Recently I watched the video of James Dobson's interview with Ted Bundy. Bundy was considered to be nothing if not a con artist, but on that particular tape I found his sincerity impressive. The interview took place only hours before his execution. Gone was the smooth, manipulative con artist who had played games with the press. Accepting full responsibility for the murders he had committed and aware of the horrendous suffering he had caused, he quietly discussed the road that eventually led him to rape and murder – a growing addiction to pornography, followed by graduation to hard-core porn. Bundy is the product of a Christian home.

We live in a society showing distinct signs of disintegration. Every month the abuse of women increases, as does the number of single mothers. In particular, change threatens the lives of children. Appalled, we wake up to the fact that sexually damaged children often grow up into sexually molesting adults, so that another generation of molesters is now growing up. And in a radically changed and sexually charged environment. Many children are damaged and many destroyed – by abortion, by abuse in the home, by sexual abuse, by parental abandonment, by satanic ritual abuse, by the horrors and hungers of street life in large cities, by death squads in Rio. In larger cities in North America, at least one boy in six and one girl in four are now molested during childhood, usually by a family member. And some statistical surveys give much higher figures than these.

The Changing Church

Throughout the period since World War II the church has been following the world, but following it at a respectable (though steadily decreasing) distance. By this I mean that changes have been taking place in the church, in its attitude and its situation.

The church knows more now than it did then about sex and shows a distinct tendency to talk about it more. But it does not talk about it anything like enough. Liberal churches pose as more enlightened than the rest of us, adjusting the categories of sin under the delusional lure of being theologically *avant garde*. Sadly, many conservative and many fundamentalist churches either remain silent on the topic of sex or else condemn sexual sins publicly but practise them secretly. Charismatic and noncharismatic churches seem equally vulnerable. We quarrel about the existence of charismatic gifts, but neither side displays (in the sexual area) the sanctifying graces.

The world is not fooled. Embarrassing disclosures of the sexual failings of prominent Christians add to the world's cynicism, not just cynicism about God's church — which would be bad enough — but about the gospel his church preaches, which is far worse. Underlying our failures is the subtle but widespread acceptance by church members of many of the world's views and sexual standards. That is not to say that the church agrees with the world. But the church reads the world's newspapers and magazines and watches the world's TV programmes. Inevitably, the world's views impact on the private feelings of church members. And it is the secret feelings of ordinary members that matter and that determine their behaviour, not public statements of official bodies. As for public statements, a number of churches have now sold out to the world.

We both flounder and founder in a sexual morass. God gave us sexuality as a refreshing lake of joy. It offers us communion – and not just to the married, since all human beings (and thus all human relationships) arise out of the fact of sex. The thrill of a grandchild's hand holding mine is not in the least erotic, yet it is a thrill arising from the procreative aspect of sex that resulted in my grandchild's existence. Had I never enjoyed sex with my wife, and had my son never enjoyed sex with his wife, this child would not be here. And now this amazing act of God's creativity clings to me. It is a wonder and delight!

Unhappily, ever since humanity fell, the lake of joy has been bordered by a foetid swamp, threaded by trails of guilt-laden pleasure. In this evil-smelling place, this place of brooding darkness and death, the church is now sinking. Church members, even church leaders, are drawn by its malign allure in increasing numbers.

A number of years ago the research department of *Christianity Today* conducted two surveys among its readers. One had to do with pastors' sexual habits and the other with the sexual failures of lay readers of the magazine. The research department mailed out nearly two thousand questionnaires, divided equally between the two groups. Only about thirty per cent of the recipients responded. One wonders why. The results confirm what some of us already knew. How would the statistics have changed, one wonders, had everybody replied? Some may have refused because they were too busy to fuss with questionnaires. Many others, I feel sure, found the material too threatening to face.

Twelve per cent of the pastors responding to the survey admitted sexual intercourse with people they related to in their pastoral work. Under the same circumstances eighteen per cent admitted to passionate kissing, fondling, mutual masturbation and so on. Such pastors regret and are troubled to make their admissions, but commonly they have nowhere to turn for help and counsel.

The *Christianity Today* statistics show that sexual failure in the pew is yet more common than that in the pulpit. The report continues, 'Incidences of immorality [among the laity] were nearly double: 45% indicated having done something sexually inappropriate, 23% said they had had extramarital intercourse, and 28% said they had engaged in other forms of extramarital sexual conduct.'[1]

Some professing Christians copulate for fun with whom they will. Our teenagers are 'sexually active.' Lonely and love-starved people snatch comfort where they can. Having bought the values of secular psychology, we claim to 'take our sexuality seriously.' We have joined the ranks of the pompously and self-righteously deceived. Slowly, looking around, we are becoming aware that along the route we have chosen we have lost our way. Church members, priests and pastors are increasingly found defending themselves against molestation charges in court.

The world at present influences the church more than the church influences the world. That is why we tumble into the morass. The fall of Christian leaders, whether local or national, once shocked and appalled us. Slowly we are beginning to take such a state of affairs for granted. Yet we need to face up to our swamp-mired condition and ask ourselves what the solution is.

Francis Frangipane, a charismatic leader in the U.S., comments, 'There are respectable men who love God and seek to serve Him, yet secretly in their hearts they are prisoners of Jezebel. Even now they are deeply ashamed of their bondage to pornography; and they can barely control their desires for women. Ask them to pray and their spirits are awash with guilt and shame. Their prayers are but the whimpers of Jezebel's eunuchs.'[2]

I Too Have Changed

Since I wrote *Eros Defiled* the church has changed, the world has changed and, along with many in my generation, I have changed. I wrote as a psychiatrist, as the pastor of a church and as the father of a young family. I now write as a grandfather and as an unofficial pastor to many younger pastors. I have seen vastly more of life as well as of sexual strugglers since I wrote *Eros Defiled*.

My views remain the same on almost everything I wrote, but in one or two matters they have changed. Though I was then aware that homosexual behaviour was wrong behaviour, I did not know God had a glorious answer for the struggler, a liberation from the torture of inversion. I will discuss the roots of inversion later in the book. Curiously, the discovery of God's ability to deliver men and women from overwhelming physical attraction to members of their own sex has brought new joys and triumphs for some gays, while other Christian gays oppose with bitter ferocity the very idea that change is possible. My views on masturbation have also undergone a significant shift. In *Eros Defiled* I described it as subnormal sexual behaviour. I now see masturbation as both sinful and psychologically damaging. I explain why in chapter five.

Most significant of all, I see sexual sin as far more important than I did at first. I had not fully realised its relationship to what Christians are now calling spiritual warfare or to the increasing violence in society. Sexual sin in the church may be the single greatest obstacle to the church's evangelistic impact on the world. Certainly our sexual enslavement is a prime goal of Satan's – a goal in which he currently enjoys enormous success.

Our evangelism is impoverished because we are under judgement. The church, believe it or not, is under judgement already. I do not speak of future judgement; I am declaring that *we are now in the midst of judgement*.

The Evolution of Judgement

The fact that the church flounders in a sexual morass and individual men and women struggle hopelessly against sexual sin is both the evidence for and a part of divine judgement. *God's principles of judgement are applied to his own people in the same way that they are applied to the world*. Ananias and Sapphira did not escape judgement. Nor did the church in Corinth. Five of the seven churches in Asia Minor were threatened with judgement unless they repented.

There is an evolution of judgement, whether in the world or among God's own people. It has always been so. Paul explains the principles in Romans 1. I discuss them in *Money Isn't God* and will do so again here.

Judgement begins long before earthquakes and 'wars and rumours of wars.' Let me express the gist of Paul's argument in Romans 1:18–32. Judgement comes in phases. One phase succeeds another. First comes intellectual and spiritual blindness, then idolatry and superstition, then loss of protection from sexual temptation of every variety, then sexual diseases, and finally a descent into total social disintegration. Only then do final judgements fall.

Phase 1 of Divine Judgement: Spiritual Blindness. If you believe a lie you come under its power. When we fail to live according to truth, a 'judicial blindness' falls on us. It is both self-imposed and God-imposed. Divine judgement begins by *giving men and women over, Christian and unbeliever alike, to whatever folly they choose*. 'For although they knew God, they neither glorified him as God nor gave thanks to him, but their thinking became futile and their foolish hearts were darkened. Although they claimed to be wise, they became fools' (Rom 1:21–22).

The sin? Knowing God but failing to glorify him. Knowing him but living lives empty of profound gratitude for the gift of life. Knowing him but accepting standards alien to Scripture, honouring ourselves and pursuing our own interests before his.

The result? The result is intellectual and spiritual blindness, the blindness of thinking we know so much, while we know nothing at all. Jesus, quoting Isaiah, affirms the phenomenon of 'judicial blindness.'

> Though seeing, they do not see; though hearing, they do not hear or understand. In them is fulfilled the prophecy of Isaiah: 'You will be ever hearing but never understanding; you will be ever seeing but never perceiving. For this people's heart has become calloused; they hardly hear with their ears, and they have closed their eyes. Otherwise they might see with their eyes, hear with their ears, understand with their hearts and turn, and I would heal them.'
>
> (Mt 13:13–15)

The terrible part of the judgement is that the spiritually blind always assume that they can see.

Phase 2: Idol Worship Is Born. The next stage is the worship of false gods. Just like the world, his own people also became fools and 'exchanged the glory of the immortal God for images made to look like mortal man and birds and animals and reptiles' (Rom 1:23).

We are not superstitious and do not bow down to idols. Instead we worship the demonic forces behind the idols directly. Our behaviour indicates that we worship money, sex and power. Therefore we have become the playthings of the gods we adore.

Phase 3: Sexual Sins and Perversions. A third stage follows rapidly. It is a further stage in our subjection to dark powers. We are 'given over' also to sexual impurity, to shameful lusts and to a depraved mind.

Therefore God *gave them over* in the sinful desires of their hearts to sexual impurity for the degrading of their bodies with one another. They exchanged the truth of God for a lie, and worshipped and served created things rather than the Creator – who is for ever praised. Amen. Because of this, *God gave them over to shameful lusts.* Even their women exchanged natural relations for unnatural ones. In the same way the men also abandoned natural relations with women and were inflamed with lust for one another. Men committed indecent acts with other men, and received in themselves the due penalty for their perversion.

(Rom 1:24–27)

Notice that vulnerability to various forms of lust and sexual perversion (and the attacks of dark powers in these forms) is here *part of the judgement.* God *gave us over*, as a community, to 'sexual impurity for the degrading of [our] bodies'! If you struggle helplessly against sexual sin, you do so because that is part of God's judgement. To put it another way, God removed his protection against sexual perversion. He let you stumble blindly along an idolatrous road of sin until you lost yourself in a maze of sexual allurement.

Far from excusing our sexual lapses, we should open our eyes to our deeper sin, the sin of not honouring God as God in the way we conduct our lives.

Phase 4: Sexual Diseases. AIDS is not a judgement of God against homosexuals or drug addicts. After all, not all people who get it are either homosexual or drug addicts. Wives and children of affected men get it. God does not protect them. In Africa and Asia AIDS is primarily a heterosexual condition, and the innocent suffer with the guilty. AIDS is a judgement of God against society – a society which God has allowed to reap a whirl-wind. AIDS has begun to invade the church, like-wise representing his judgement. It is the result of the same sin, the sin of failing to honour God as he should be honoured in our lives. Society and the church have been given over to the inevitable sequence – to unnatural sex, subsequently reaping 'the due penalty for their perversion' (Rom 1:27).

Thus in the evolution of judgement, first comes blindness, then the sexual insanity into which our pride has led us. And it is the sexual insanity that is the real judgement.

Phase 5: Satanic Defiance. The last five verses of Romans 1 describe the penultimate stage of earthly judgement. They present an appalling picture. Yet it is a picture of human behaviour that we see all around us.

> Furthermore, *since they did not think it worth-while to retain the knowledge of God, he gave them over to a depraved mind*, to do what ought not to be done. They have become filled with every kind of wickedness, evil, greed and depravity. They are full of envy, murder, strife, deceit and malice. They are gossips, slanderers, God-haters, insolent, arrogant and boastful; they invent ways of doing evil; they disobey their parents; they are senseless, faithless, heartless, ruthless. *Although they know God's righteous decree that those who do such things deserve death*, they not only continue to do these very

things but also approve of those who practise them.

(Rom 1:28–32)

I have italicised two phrases in the passage. Both
re-emphasise the point Paul insists on. Blindness
to the things of God is a blindness for which
all human beings in every part of the globe are
responsible. At that point God *gives us over* to
the consequences of our choices. Then come the
wars and catastrophes, which are today already
quickening in their tempo.

God never loses his love for sinners, be their sin
sexual promiscuity, perversion or whatever form.
Jesus once said, '"I desire mercy, not sacrifice." For
I have not come to call the righteous, but sinners'
(Mt 9:13).

Real repentance is a profound work of God. I
write about it in chapter ten. It begins with the
illumination of the Holy Spirit as he removes the
blindness, that strange spiritual insanity that is
the first stage in judgement. It radically affects
emotions, conscience, will. It is a new 'seeing'
that changes our attitudes about and our feelings
toward God and sin.[3]

Is Doom Inevitable?

Is there no hope?

Away with the very idea! A Day of Deliverance
has arrived. God is doing things today that fill
me with joy and wonder. I write of redemption
as well as doom – redemption from chains, from
bondage. If I spend time dealing with the horror
of our condition, I do so because the glory of our
deliverance and of our Deliverer is thereby seen

more clearly. Our God triumphs. He triumphs both in his judgements and in his deliverance.

Be certain, then, of one thing. Darkness will never overcome light. The smallest candle drives darkness from the largest auditorium. The only way to let darkness conquer you is by turning your back on light.

I invite you to walk with me, from the darkness and into the light.

The Uniqueness of Sexual Sin

We have seen that sexual sin is epidemic in the church. How did the epidemic arise? It arose because the powers of darkness have their own agenda for church life. Satan goes for sex first. His strategy has always stressed control over a people's sexual mores. Ever since our forefathers discovered the shame and embarrassment of their nakedness, the satanic strategy of making sexual sin a prime goal has steadily become more apparent in biblical and cultural history.

Sociologists and psychologists might offer us descriptive theories of sin's grip, but they would be just that – *descriptions*, not true explanations. For explanations we turn to Scripture. We must start to understand by grasping the biblical fact that sexual sin is unique.

Paul's statement in 1 Corinthians 6:18 is startling: 'All other sins a man commits are outside his body, but he who sins sexually sins against his own body.' He says that sexual sin differs from all other sin. The words 'all other sins' clearly imply a distinction between sins that gratify sexual lust and every other sin in the book. Sexual sin is different. This is why Paul tells us to flee from it

– to take flight, shun it, run from it. It is different, he says, different *because it does something to our own bodies*. The argument makes little sense at first. What does Paul mean?

The Bible nowhere says sexual sin is *morally worse* than other sins. Pride is the worst sin of all. In the words of C.S. Lewis, pride is the sin that made Satan Satan. Scripture deplores cruelty and violence more than wrongful sex. Yet the church throughout the centuries has recognised that in some distinctive way sexual sin is a sin to be shunned. Why?

If we are to understand why and in what way lewdness is a special case, we shall need to understand how Paul thinks. Being Jewish, he thinks like his Jewish contemporaries. He differs from most of us in two ways: in his *anthropology*, his view of what a human being is, and in his *historiography*, his understanding of the significance of Jewish history.

Pauline Anthropology

How does Paul view our humanity? In particular, how does he view the human body and sexuality?

His view is that marriage is good and the body is good. The marriage bed is undefiled. The body is God-created, God-redeemed. It logically follows that the sexual parts of our bodies and the feelings they give rise to are a gift from God. He designed them, gave them to us. Therefore we must bless him for our sexual parts and sexual feelings. The hearty and grateful acceptance of our sexuality is an essential step in overcoming lust.

Notice what a high view Paul has of the human

body. Eight times in 1 Corinthians 6 from verse 13 to verse 20 the term *body* occurs. Each mention is devoted to showing its glory.

More to the point, God the Son *currently exists in a human body*, uniting our human condition with divinity. He will remain so throughout eternity.

Pauline Historiography

Later in 1 Corinthians (10:1–10) Paul offers a quick review of the history of Israel following their exodus from Egypt under Moses' leadership. 'For I do not want you to be ignorant of . . . our forefathers' he begins, for they committed many sins as they wandered in the wilderness and died there as a result. Then, he draws his conclusions. 'Do not be idolaters, as some of them were; as it is written: "The people sat down to eat and drink and got up to indulge in pagan revelry." We should not commit sexual immorality, as some of them did – and in one day twenty-three thousand of them died' (1 Cor 10:1, 7–8).

Paul's mention of twenty-three thousand who died is a reference to a very significant incident in the history of Israel that occurred at Shittim. In *Eros Redeemed* I look more closely at this episode to understand the uniqueness of sexual sin, considering several key concepts: (1) The incident at Shittim as a turning point in Israel's history; (2) the role and nature of pagan fertility religions and their impact on Israel; (3) genocide and divine judgement; and (4) Satan's territorial claims on earth. However, in this book I shall omit such considerations.

Fertility Cults

The pagan world into which Israel was moving worshipped fertility.

God had made it clear that he alone was the only source of life, fertility and prosperity (Deut 7:13–16). He alone made crops grow and animals reproduce. Only he gave rain. Locust armies were under his control. Fertility was a gift of his grace. In making sex a mysterious ritual (the seed of your body in exchange for the multiplication of your crops), the fertility religions revived Satan's rivalry with heaven. Other sins might involve other forms of idolatry and be 'outside the body' (1 Cor 6:18). Sexual sin always involves the presentation of one's body (and therefore also of our whole selves) to the dark powers that wish to control it.

Like certain other sins, sexual sin grips. It tends to be repetitive, compulsive. I have heard experienced Christian leaders say, 'Once a pastor has fallen into sexual sin, you will never be able to trust him again.' I believe they are wrong, but I admit that healing and repentance must precede restoration to service.

The element that psychology and psychiatry miss in sinful compulsions is satanic power and control. Sexual sinners are under the control of darkness, not because it is more evil than other sins but because we are more easily controlled by sex. Hence its strategic significance in warfare. This may be more true of men than of women. Get your hands on a man's genitals, and you can do almost anything with him.

The fact that we lose control, finding ourselves hopelessly and helplessly in the grip of sexual

urges now inflamed by satanic cohorts, is no
excuse. We are responsible for the sexual sins
we commit. We got ourselves into the mess by our
own choice. Drunk drivers are responsible for the
death of anyone they slaughter on the highway.
Likewise, child molesters are accountable for the
cruel wrong to their victims. We are to be held
accountable for every sexual sin we commit. If we
are the victims of dark powers, it is because we
have chosen to be. (See Rom 1:20–25.)

And what does all this have to do with the
church's victory over the powers of darkness now?
Just this – that temptation to sexual sin is Satan's
first stratagem in impairing our ability to fight.
We preach the gospel to a lost world with our
shield arms tied behind our backs and our ears
deaf to divine orders.

Judgement and a God of Love

Let us face facts. The God of the Scriptures is
both tender and fierce, just as the Jesus of the
New Testament was by turns torn by compassion
and filled with flaming ferocity. Judgement fell
on Israel many times. God knows the deadly
nature of sin. We *have no concept of the danger,
the horrendous deadliness of sin, and therefore
judgement bewilders us.*

Chapter 2

Overcoming Sexual Sin

*Some tree, whose broad smooth leaves, together sewed,
And girded on our loins, may cover round
Those middle parts, that this new comer, Shame,
There sit not, and reproach us as unclean.*
JOHN MILTON, PARADISE LOST

*How could one man chase a thousand, or two put ten
thousand to flight, unless their Rock had sold them,
unless the LORD had given them up? . . . Their vine
comes from the vine of Sodom and from the fields of
Gomorrah. Their grapes are filled with poison, and
their clusters with bitterness.*
DEUTERONOMY 32:30, 32

Satan seized on our sexuality during human
history's opening moments, covering us with
shame at our own bodies. In doing so he polluted
and distorted sex.

Sex happens to be one means by which we learn
to relate intimately.[1] I do not speak merely of brief
moments of sexual ecstasy, for learning intimacy
takes a lifetime – a lifetime of fidelity, of self-
discovery and of the discovery of someone else.

Was Satan jealous that God should confer so
high a privilege on time-bound, warm-blooded,
naked bipeds?

Whatever the reason, Satan not only went for our sexuality when time began but has made it a prime means of control over humanity ever since.

God and Evil

God controls all things. He sets limits on evil beings – angels, demons, humans. I like the King James version of Psalm 76:10: 'Surely the wrath of man shall praise thee: the remainder of wrath shalt thou restrain.' God uses evil that flows from the Fall and from our own sin to bring judgement to pass. Thus disaster, disease, darkness and death come about by the choices of evil men and women, and by the powers of evil.

Satan is the immediate author of catastrophe. We sow the evil wind and we reap an evil whirlwind. Satan sends hurricanes, earthquakes, wars, plagues, famine. He does so within the hand of the God of judgement and holiness. The evil comes from Satan – but only within a God-created universe that allows real choices and real consequences to exist. So Paul the apostle receives 'a messenger of Satan to buffet him.' And because God has a good purpose in the buffeting, God ignores Paul's pleading to be delivered. God turns evil to good.

Satan has usurped earthly rule. God allowed this when he cursed the earth. We had to learn the nature of our choice by experience. Now the earth produces thorns and briars which were not part of the original creation. It also produces sickness and death. It is cursed. It is ruled by demons. It is a place of perpetual struggle against alienation.

I can only presume that evil powers do not comprehend the extent to which they fulfil the divine purposes! They do so insofar as God uses them in bringing about divine judgement. It is God's overall goal to eliminate them. In doing so he uses mankind – specifically his ancient people and the church.

The Nature of Idolatry

So we return to Israel. Prior to the incident at Shittim, (Num 25:1–5, 8–9) God was preparing Israel to be the nation through whom the world's Deliverer would come. It is to become a nation free from any form of idolatry, occupying territory free from territorial claim by the fertility gods. The very ground has been polluted and must now be cleansed. Moses makes it clear that they are to be the instruments of judgement on those nations through whom territorial claim was exercised. They are to fight. On one level the battles are to be fought in time and space, with swords, spears, arrows and human determination to obey the God of Israel. On another level it will be a battle in the heavenlies, as human beings take part in celestial warfare by their faith and their obedience. Worship and idolatry are to be key issues.

The Israelites were in step with the Spirit. They were the recipients of divine instructions, given to Moses by God. They would form an instrument in God's hands to come against the powers of darkness, to aim at their destruction. The Israelites were to eliminate idolatry in the countries they conquered.

What exactly *is* idolatry? It is false worship – worship of beings other than God, who alone merits worship. In the case of Israel and the surrounding nations it was worship by sex, by

penis, by vagina. Worship is to give to something
or someone else what belongs exclusively to God.
In practice, it is also to 'exchange the truth of God
for a lie.' Idolatry, then, must be understood by
contrasting it with true worship.

To worship God, the God of Creation, is to know
why we were born. At its lowest level worship is
a deeply satisfying duty. It can be much more –
it can be warfare or even ecstasy. Yet neither as
duty, nor as warfare, nor yet as ecstasy does it
have meaning if the basis of the worship is absent.
Worship begins to arise when we hear the word
of the Lord and respond to it. Our response is
worship and reveals a trusting heart. Trust issues
in obedience. *Unless we are those who hear God's
word and obey it, our worship is meaningless*.

To hear the word of the Lord and do it is
automatically to present our bodies not to dark
powers but to the Lord as a living sacrifice. The
moment you do God's will, you do it with your
body. You let him use that body. The two things
are one and the same. As Paul said, 'Therefore,
I urge you, brothers, in view of God's mercy, to
offer your bodies as living sacrifices, holy and
pleasing to God – this is your *spiritual act of
worship*' (Rom 12:1).

Just as the basis of worship is to hear the word
of the Lord and do it (thus presenting our bodies to
God in worship), so idolatry is to hear the words of
darkness and to act on them (thus presenting our
bodies to the powers of darkness in worship). It is
to trust the word and the wisdom of darkness. It is,
I repeat, to present your body a living sacrifice to
certain powers of darkness, which is exactly what
Adam and Eve did. They listened to the serpent's
word and acted upon it.

Worship begins with trust and obedience. We have been 'rescued . . . from the dominion of darkness and brought . . . into the kingdom of the Son' (Col 1:13). Yet as we fall into idolatrous practices we cross the line again, choosing the dominion of darkness from which God rescued us. Where does the deepest essence of idolatry lie?

Idolatry is to hear the word of darkness, to trust it and to do it. Paul is under no misapprehension about the spiritual forces involved in idolatry. 'Do I mean then that a sacrifice offered to an idol is anything, or that an idol is anything? No, but the sacrifices of pagans are offered to demons, not to God, and I do not want you to be participants with demons. You cannot drink the cup of the Lord and the cup of demons too; you cannot have a part in both the Lord's table and the table of demons' (1 Cor 10:19–21).

Worship begins when we hear the word of the Lord and do it. Idolatry begins when we listen to the word of darkness and do it. In Israel's case the word of darkness had to do with certain sexual practices. But before I leave the subject of images, let me emphasise that we must never forget the demon behind the image.

The idol is not at the core of idolatry. Other actions link us more closely to certain false gods.

Should any doubt remain that the essence of idolatry lies in the action that God hates (the sexuality involved in certain forms of idolatry), let us look back at God's words through Moses: 'And after they [the nations inhabiting the Promised Land] have been destroyed before you, be careful not to be ensnared by inquiring about their gods, saying, "How do these nations serve their gods? We will do the same." *You must not worship the LORD*

*your God in their way, because in worshipping
their gods, they do all kinds of detestable things
the LORD hates'* (Deut 12:30–31).

'They do all kinds of detestable things.' We may
claim to worship the true God by asserting that
we do not bow down before any images, or by
claiming the most correct theology. But if we
are heeding dark words and defending immoral
practices, doing 'all kinds of detestable things,'
then our worship is not acceptable. We must never
worship our God in this way. Far more important
than the bowing to an idol is the detestable
practice associated with the worship.

Imagery and 'the Word of Darkness'

I have spoken several times about listening to
dark words. Dark words seduce us by the images
they evoke. I mentioned that Eve, in the garden,
was so lured. What is 'the word of darkness'? In the
case of sexual sin it may run something like this:

'God knows how your husband neglects you and
makes you suffer. Why not give yourself to this
other man who understands you so and shows you
such tenderness?'

Or, 'God made you the way you are. Celebrate
your gayness and thank him. Do the thing that is
in your heart!'

Or, 'There's no harm in it. This magazine is an
art form. Human bodies are beautiful. God gave us
sex to enjoy. (But don't upset your wife by showing
the stuff to her!)'

Or, 'If you really love him (or her), keep doing
it. It's okay. Why all the fuss about a marriage
certificate? Your heart tells you the sex you had
last night was holy.'

When you accept and follow such words you do exactly what Eve did. You hear darkness and put its advice to work. You turn your face from God. You enter delusion and darkness. In so doing, you place yourself under the sovereignty of darkness. Your body is offered as a living sacrifice to the old fertility gods. And you may be sure that your offering will be accepted with delight. You will not thereby lose your salvation, but you will experience loss of self-control. You will lose the earthly experience of Christ's blood-bought deliverance from sexual sin.

Devoted Things

So important was it to break the territorial power of the fertility gods that God at times instructed the Israelites to eliminate not only all human inhabitants from an area, but animals as well. Even the artifacts of the civilization were to be destroyed. Usually metal was to be melted down and then devoted to God. Occasionally animals did not need to be destroyed.

Whatever faced destruction was referred to as *devoted* – devoted to destruction. Or, better, everything was to be devoted to God, some things for destruction, a little of it, once purged, for his service. Thus as Israel stood ready to take Jericho, Joshua cried, 'Shout! For the LORD has given you the city! The city and all that is in it are to be *devoted to the* LORD' (Josh 6:16–17). That which was not devoted to God for his use was to be devoted on his behalf to destruction.

We cannot do warfare with the powers of darkness when we play around with devoted things. God will no longer fight with us. 'I will not be with

you any more unless you destroy whatever among
you is devoted to destruction' (Josh 7:12).

What are devoted things in our case? Surely
the lesson is plain! If articles of clothing, simple
articles, were to be destroyed, how much more the
sins that were associated with their use? Any form
of sexual sin is a devoted thing. Why should it
surprise us that the world shows no interest in
the gospel? The church is filled with men, women
and young people who cleave to devoted things.

The solution? 'Go, consecrate the people. Tell
them, "Consecrate yourselves in preparation for
tomorrow; for this is what the LORD, the God of
Israel, says: That which is devoted is among you,
O Israel. *You cannot stand against your enemies
until you remove it*"' (Josh 7:13).

We are to remove sin, and especially sexual sin.
The task of eliminating it from the church may
seem impossible. Nothing is impossible with God.
The day of mercy is upon us. We are commanded
to consecrate ourselves. Let us begin at once
to do so.

The problem

In this section of the book we are trying to understand the problem – the problem of the effect
of the Fall on our experience. The sections that
follow will deal with the interaction of Bible and
theology and with our redemption, God's answer
to the problem of sexual sin. Before we get into
psychological and redemptive aspects, however,
we need to look more carefully at a major social
consequence of sexual promiscuity – violence in a
society. We will do this in the next chapter.

Chapter 3

Sexual Sin and Violence

There are six things the LORD hates, seven that are detestable to him: haughty eyes, a lying tongue, hands that shed innocent blood.
PROVERBS 6:16–17

I start this chapter, not with sexual sin, but with the sequence of social changes that Paul tells us will inevitably follow in any society — whether among God's people or not. I include this because I feel an urgency about the present situation. It cannot go on. It must not. Judgement hangs over us, and I must cry out whether I am heard or not.

You will recall that Paul describes the changes that follow sexual sin in Romans 1:18–32. The sequence begins with our not allowing God to have his place among us (vv 18–20). Then follow darkness and idolatry (vv 21–23), then sexual sin and sexual perversion (vv 24–27), and finally a totally corrupt and disintegrating society of people who have been given over by God 'to a depraved mind, to do what ought not to be done' (vv 28–32).

History records repeated occurrences of this grim sequence. It is my contention that we are fast getting to the climax of another cycle in the

world as a whole, and we in the church are not too
far behind. I point this out so that we, the church,
may begin to face the fact of sexual sin in our
midst now, lest we reap the full consequences –
those divine judgements that began with the Flood
and continued with catastrophic events in the life
of Israel.

Prominent among the features of the abandoned
society Paul describes is violence. The people affected by the process wind up full of murder and strife
(v 29). Such people are referred to as heartless and
ruthless (v 31). The society began to change once
they had been given over to sexual impurity (v
24). Later we can look at a few statistics but I
propose to look at Scripture first since I believe
we need some sort of screen, a lens through
which to gaze at and assess the world. Why is
this necessary?

In *U.S. News and World Report*, John Leo
comments on a question Marshall McLuhan used
to ask: 'If the temperature of the bath water rises
one degree every ten minutes, how will the bather
know when to scream? (Frogs don't! They allow
themselves to be boiled.)'

Leo is quoting McLuhan to draw attention to
an article by Senator Daniel Patrick Moynihan.
The article, 'Defining Deviancy Down,' is about
our tendency to pretend something catastrophic
is not happening when in fact it is. Leo says,
'Moynihan doesn't use the word *pretend*. He uses
the psychological word *denial* and the sociologi-
cal word *normalizing*, but they amount to the
same thing. By normalizing he means that some
excruciatingly hot bath water is now accepted as
a normal, everyday feature of American life.'[1]

And not only of American life, but of the

life of the whole Western world, not to mention the Western church. But because terms are redefined constantly ('illegitimate birth' becomes 'out-of-wedlock birth,' then 'single parenting') and because statistics are not 'hard' but 'soft' and easy to manipulate, we need a clarifying biblical lens to look through. So what about violence? What does Scripture say? Remember, I am looking at violence in one way only – as a sort of flag to indicate whether the many characteristics of the abandoned society now surround *us*.

The Biblical Perspective

The Bible shows repeatedly the sequence which Paul describes. The terrible shame of nakedness in Genesis 3 is followed in Genesis 4 by the first murder. Cain murders Abel. The scriptural sequence from that point on may be 'explained' in a whole variety of different ways. That is not my point. We are not looking at explanations but at the sequence Paul describes in terms of divine judgement. Any explanation in terms of psychology, sociology or any of the human sciences is irrelevant. For in judgement God begins by progressively removing his hand of mercy and restraint from our behaviour, allowing us to become subject to the sequence of Romans 1. The sequence has a spiritual, not a scientific, explanation. It obeys not human laws but divine ones.

Genesis 3–4 is followed by Genesis 6, where unnatural sex is mentioned. 'The Nephilim were on the earth in those days – and also afterwards – when the sons of God went to the daughters of men and had children by them' (Gen 6:4). And the result? 'The LORD saw how great man's

wickedness on the earth had become, and that
every inclination of the thoughts of his heart was
only evil all the time' (v. 5). What sort of evil? 'Now
the earth was corrupt in God's sight *and was full
of violence*' (v. 11).

The sequence continues throughout the Old Testament: sexual sin, then violence. What effect of
the sex-soaked idolatry figures most prominently
in prophetic denunciations? Violence and abuse of
the fatherless, the widow, the aged, the poor. 'Do
no wrong or violence to the alien, the fatherless or
the widow, and do not shed innocent blood in this
place' (Jer 22:3).

Once sexual sin starts in a given society, violence follows. David the king has sex with Uriah's
wife. (Phase 1: sexual sin.) Then, after doing
his best to cover the sin, he arranges to have
Uriah murdered. (Phase 2: violence.) David has
forgotten (or else no longer cares) that Uriah bears
God's image.

We protest: 'This one doesn't count!' We say, 'Don't
you understand? The affair would have become public otherwise. That is the *real* explanation.'

Our explanations are irrelevant. Judgement,
not motivation, is the central issue here. A man
who has 'borrowed' another man's wife finds himself committing an even more appalling crime
before he has time to think clearly. His mind
had been darkened even before he committed
adultery. He had become lazy, idle. So he sowed
the wind and reaped a whirlwind before he came
to his senses. One example of this same sequence
is common today. Illicit sex followed by unwanted
pregnancy and abortion. Phase 1: sex. Phase 2:
abortion. They are links in the chain, part of an
overall sequence.

All of these examples, whether inside or outside Scripture, can be explained in the deepest sense only in the light of Romans 1. God *gives us over* to sexual impurity (v. 24), then to the shameful lust of homosexuality (v. 26), and finally to a depraved mind to do whatever things we choose to (vv. 28–32). Prominent among these is violent behaviour.

Do statistics bear this out? Might we be reaching yet another climax (or rather, low point) at the present time?

Is Violence Growing?

'According to the UCR [the compilation and analysis by the FBI of all reported crimes] violence in the United States has increased in the past ten years . . . the violence rate increased 25 percent . . . the rate of rapes more than 15 percent and assaults more than 47 percent . . . In 1991 . . . the number of murders topped 24,000 for the first time in the nation's history.'[2]

Curiously, the increase in violence does not correspond to the general crime rate. 'Unlike violent crime, property crime has remained relatively stable during the past decade.'[3] Is the United States more violent than other countries? 'According to the Senate Judiciary Committee on violence, the United States is "the most violent and self-destructive nation on earth." The committee reports that . . . the U.S. murder rate is four times as great as Italy's, nine times England's and twice that of Northern Ireland.'[4]

I am not competent to discuss these trends and will not make the attempt. Perhaps the hotly debated issue of the availability of weapons has some bearing on the question. The real question is: Does a sword of divine judgement hang over North America?

And what about other nations, especially Western nations?

Trends in Western Nations

It is trends that matter, not the amount of violence in a given country. The question everywhere is: Is violence on the increase? The United States may be a special case with an exaggerated proneness to violence.

Let me cut across a country-by-country analysis of violence trends and focus on war. One difficulty is to define war. The traditional approach centres around distinctions between civil wars within a country and wars affecting more than one nation. But the difficulties do not stop there. Students of war demand a comprehensive theoretical framework.

But in the minds of those who fight, rather than clearcut theories there is a wild range of emotions. And violence begins with the emotions that eventually drive you to it. Wars begin when political leaders experience a degree of rage or fear or a combination of both.

Within all of us is a curious mixture of the divine image and satanic corruption. War is not simple. Only violence itself can be quantified. But how? On any reading of the evidence, armed conflict – both between nations and within national boundaries – has increased. From Uppsala University comes the statement that 'the total number of armed conflicts in the world in 1990 were 82, and in 1991 71.'[5] The fact that there were fewer in 1991 does not reflect a 'downward trend' but merely a dip in this awful state of affairs.

A seething subsurface anger is what feeds modern wars. Inner rage, especially between ethnic groups, boils in the masses throughout the globe as I write. Deny it and you will be blind to the catastrophic judgement that is on the way. There is no question as to what is to follow, though I have no timetable to offer. Romans 1 remains the lens through which to view the international scene.

Chapter 4

Satanic Sex

Our interpretation is a thing we bring to history and superimpose upon it . . . Therefore, the liberal, the Jesuit, the Fascist, the Communist, and all the rest may sail away with their militant versions of history, howling at one another across the interstellar spaces, all claiming theirs is the absolute version.
HERBERT BUTTERFIELD

Allegations of child sexual abuse often disturb people in a way that elicits the age-old human response of wanting to shoot the messenger who brings the bad news. People find it more comfortable to believe that children are natural liars.
KEVIN MARRON

I sense that Mephistopheles is still grinning.
WALTER SUNDBERG

Do Satanists and witches exist? Do they subject children to terrible abuse? Does satanic sex exist? Is there any such thing? A debate rages currently over these questions. We are faced by two sets of people – some who claim to be victims of it and who give dramatic stories of the way it has wrecked their lives, and others who are sceptics, who declare they have investigated the stories and no solid evidence for their truth exists. Christians and non-Christians are found in both groups. In the face of the debate, how can we determine who is correct? How do we discover the facts? Is there any smoke behind this fire?

The Controversy

Some believe that children are being ritually brutalised and sometimes killed in satanic sacrificial offerings. For example, Cynthia Kisser, executive director of the Cult Awareness Network, quotes many decisions by highly authoritative and responsible bodies who show concern about Satanism.

However, Jeffrey Victor, a human sexuality expert, sets the tone for an article he wrote in the winter 1992/93 issue of the journal *Free Inquiry* by quoting Ben Yehuda's 1920 remark that 'sometimes societies create imaginary forms of deviance in order to have scapegoats for deep social and political tensions.' Such is the case, he feels, with the current concern over Satanism. He states that the 'satanic-cult scare is . . . a witch-hunt for moral "subversives" and supposed criminals in a highly secretive conspiratorial network.'[1]

The Core of the Matter

On both sides it is basically a matter of belief, even though writers talk in terms of 'scientific evidence' or even 'proof.' We are faced with a situation where large numbers of people are convinced of diametrically opposed viewpoints about reality. Not only so, but professions are divided on the issues. There are social workers, psychologists, psychiatrists, police, lawyers, judges, journalists and politicians on both sides of the debate.

Both sides are discussing Satanism. However
we must turn our attention not to Satanism but
to Satan; not to a human conspiracy but to a plot
hatched by dark supernatural beings. Do they
exist? Does Satan exist? If so, how active is he
on earth? If dark powers are active, it should not
surprise us that some people might worship them,
or even that the number of worshippers might be
on the increase. After all, witches have been his-
torically very much a part of the human scene.

Balance

Debates often shift the centre of interest away
from a larger problem. The evil of satanic ritual
abuse (SRA) pales before a greater evil, the evil of
the sexual abuse of children by people far removed
from witchcraft. This of course is where our main
concern should lie. We must see the debate in the
context of brutality against these children, of child
sexual abuse in the home, the church and the
community. While in the current climate of panic
false accusations are being made, real child abuse
is very common. Incest and domestic violence are
growing. The number of prosecutions is rising.

The abuse I experienced as an eleven-year-
old from a Christian worker makes me sensitive
about this. My abuser may have been satanically
inspired, but he was not a Satanist. (Yet is the
stride from satanically inspired sexual abuse to
witchcraft and Satanism such a long one?)

Incest is undoubtedly numerically commoner
than the more bizarre and dramatic SRA. It is
also more serious, in that it is often perpetrated
by professing Christian parents, grandparents

and other relatives and predators, some of whom struggle vainly against their proclivity, hiding it. Most churches are helpless to deal with the problem. It is this that reminds us that the powers of darkness are behind the church's apparent irrelevance. Satan and his rabble are alive and increasing in power, while many churches seem unaware of their danger.

Therefore, when we think of SRA we must see it as part of a larger pattern. Satan is behind the emerging pattern, damaging the lives of children in their own homes, commonly homes of the 'respectable' variety, but also homes of parents who practise witchcraft.

Earlier I stressed that it was not Satanism but Satan and demons that must interest us. Another reason for the scepticism of some Christians may be that they have never experienced a live demon. To believe demons exist is one thing. To meet one is quite another. And when I talk of meeting a demon, I am not talking about a subjective experience that no one else can verify, but about a dramatic manifestation of a demonic presence in someone in whom such a thing had never previously taken place, and that was totally unexpected – by me, by the victims and by other observers who were present.

To have such experiences is suddenly to be aware that one is surrounded by other worlds, other beings, other powers. In my case the awareness fades quickly, for the influence of the material world of Newtonian science is so much a part of my background and training – and, as Lewis puts it, a good dose of 'real life' quickly dispels the feeling of surrounding angels and demons. I am not a 'natural' believer. But the repeated demonic manifestations that occur when I approach demonized persons, or when I pray for someone, not knowing they are demonized, restores my belief.

Sex, Sacrifice and Sorcery in Scripture

In Scripture the idolatry of the fertility cults, witchcraft and sorcery all were part and parcel of one another. We may not make sacrifices to idols today, but as I have already made clear, we are into the same thing without the superstition. Let me then begin with Scripture and with the reminder that witchcraft used to accompany the fertility cults, with their associated child sacrifice and ritual sex. It existed in the Old Testament and the New. I must establish this clearly. I know this does not prove that it still exists. Nor does it, in itself, prove that witchcraft had (and has) access to satanic power. But it does establish a more-than-occasional social relationship between these things. Satan may shuffle his cards a little, using sleight of hand to shove in an ace of agnosticism (in respect to idolatry), but he retains the same essential hand.

The Importance of Knowing What to Expect

Perhaps many of the supposed victims are victims of their own imagination. On the other hand, the fact that I wear biblical spectacles means I shall not be surprised if hideously damaged victims of witchcraft should cross my path more than occasionally. Wearing the spectacles I do, I shall expect to find witchcraft and sorcery increasing wherever sex is worshipped and violence rises.

Sorcery was a natural companion of pagan idolatry. Following the Reformation, the naturalist philosophical movements on the European continent, and the empiricism of philosophers like Hume, Berkeley and Locke, together with the growth of empiricist science, all tended to diminish the importance of witchcraft in the public mind. It was at that time diminished just in the same way as it had previously been exaggerated.

Now the pendulum is swinging rapidly to the other extreme. When this happens it always swings too far. At the moment we are near the apex of the swing. But there is never smoke without a fire. So far as I am concerned, the bizarre nature of the practices of witchcraft allow me neither to raise my eyebrows nor to shrug my shoulders. We must ask God to give us enough experience and discernment not to relish the latest wild story as proof of our beliefs. We need to cry to him for wisdom about where the truth lies in a given case, for there are many exploiters of attention and pity who are only too willing to lead us down some garden path of their own creating.

Smoke and Fire

It is true that if you are suddenly presented with someone's story, and the story depends on the subjective evidence of the person who tells the story, there is not much to go on. But there are things you cannot fake, hard evidence that frequently accompanies real victims. It consists of anal and vaginal scarring. And there are doctors who testify about examinations that bear out these facts. When the findings are combined with memories and nightmares, one then knows one has a genuine example of satanic ritual abuse.

I have no doubt that SRA exists. The debate should centre around how common it is. Satanic ritual abuse is cruel abuse, mostly of infants and young children, who grow accustomed to it and assume there is nothing wrong with it. It commonly goes unnoticed by professionals dealing with childhood sexual abuse simply because they are unaware of its existence, or, if aware, they have little idea of its extent. What you don't expect, you do not look for. Police and the courts were initially cynical, especially since some early reports of it could not be substantiated.[2]

What we need to grasp is that men and particularly women who are victims of such abuse earlier in their lives will be turning in increasing numbers to Christians for help during the next few years. Among them there may be manipulative attention seekers, so we will need discernment and spiritual power to help effectively. The damage done to small children in their early years can have appalling effects in later life, psychologically, spiritually and socially.

What we must never forget is that few people have any experience of dealing with victims of witchcraft, behind which lies all the malice of Satan toward God. We are fools to believe we are qualified to enter into such a conflict in our own wisdom; we must recognise our need for and continued dependence on the Holy Spirit for discernment.

Cases are coming to light with increasing frequency. Police are taking note of what is happening, gradually assuming a more responsible attitude. Their effectiveness is limited for many reasons. After all, how able are they to contain even the drug problem? The rising crime rate? Hampered by lack of personnel, they will never stamp our Satanism. More significantly, they will never do so because they are fighting spiritual powers with human weapons.

Ken Blue[3] warned a police officer in our area, whose assignment was to investigate witchcraft and Satanism, that without Christ he was in great danger. Shortly afterwards that police officer took his own life.

The Emergence of the Occult

Suddenly a number of churches are finding themselves facing what the church down the ages has faced – the powerful reality of witchcraft. It should not surprise us if our sex-sated and violence-crazed society should turn out to be seething with sorcery. Both are manifestations of Satan's rule on earth.

The Nature of Christian Warfare

This is the day of God's mercy to sinners in society – and in the church. Our main weapon in the battle with the powers of darkness is the gospel. We are not called on to rule society as a Christian elite, nor even to reform society. We are called to obey Christ, and in so doing to allow the Holy Spirit to awaken society to its peril, causing large segments of it to turn in repentance and faith to God. When that happens society will be reformed. Our aim, however, is not societal reformation, but the declaration of the kingdom of God which divides society with the sword of truth.

Our main task is not even to tackle or take on the powers of darkness. We will inevitably be at war with them if we are effective in obeying Christ. To be sure, we need to know something about their methods of warfare. But they themselves are not our main assignment. Our main assignment is the rescue and redemption of perishing human beings. Our goal is to reach a lost world, to carry out the Great Commission.

The church, though an army, is at this point a badly battered army with many wounded. Many church members are compromised, unable to fight. We have secretly kept *devoted things* for ourselves, and therefore we are constantly defeated in battles with dark powers. I believe many churches have an unwritten understanding with the powers of darkness: 'We'll leave you alone if you'll leave us alone.'

The Day of Deliverance

In the mercy of God, this is the day in which God is dealing with sexual sin and violence among his own people. This is the day in which we renounce our idols and the pseudodeities behind them. This is the day in which we forsake idolatry and return to God.

How do I know that the day of God's deliverance has arrived? The first time I fully expounded the material I deal with in chapter one in a European country, the effects were startling. I rarely make an appeal and never a long one. All I ever say – *and I say it only once* – is, 'If you wish to acknowledge your sin and need prayer for help, come forward!' Then I wait. If no one comes – fine.

On that occasion in Europe, young men began to *run* forward. Soon an avalanche of people, men, women, young, old, broke loose, making hurry impossible by the density with which they crowded together. Of four thousand Christian leaders present, an estimated two thousand five hundred pushed forward, seeking prayer for unavailing struggles against their sex drives. The majority were members of conservative churches. Before long, we began to hear the agonised cries of desperate men and women and the shrieks of demons.

These reactions owe nothing to any ability I personally may have. They are the result of both the working of the Spirit and the victory of the Son of God. God is making men and women desperate and opening wide the door to repentance and hope. The effects have not always been quite so dramatic, though the material on violence (which is, I believe, the inevitable social consequence of sexual promiscuity) shows some astonishing effects. In the meantime we have become better equipped to deal with large numbers of people needing prayer and counsel for sexual sin.

We have also taken care to discourage people from coming forward unless they know that God has spoken to them. Recently in a meeting of over three thousand Christian people (including a high proportion of pastors and Christian leaders), almost one-third came forward to acknowledge and seek help for their inability to control rage and, in the case of some, violence in the home. Those confessing their need of help were conducted to two large rooms where they could receive extensive prayer and help. Again, large numbers of demons spontaneously manifested themselves.[4]

Unless and until the church faces up to her need for deliverance from sexual sin and violence in the home *and deals with that need*, the power of God will not be on the church's evangelism in the way it could be. But the power of God is on the church at this moment to deal with sex and violence. We live in the day of Christ's deliverance. Powerful as the dark powers may be, they are no match for their Creator and our Redeemer, who is in our midst to save us all from the tyrannies that have held sway for too long.

The moment we start to 'clean up our act,' the warfare will begin. Yet unless and until churches clean up immorality and violence among their members, they will remain in darkness, ignorant of their blindness. Their successes in battle will be minor and their defeats major. Fine buildings, excellent programmes, highly trained pastors are all relatively unimportant in comparison with dealing with the hidden skeletons in our closets.

It is with this task in mind that I write.

Chapter 5

The Marriage of Sex and Love

There dwell an accursed people, full of pride and lust. There when a man takes a maiden in marriage they do not lie together, but each lies with a cunningly fashioned image of the other.
C.S. LEWIS, THAT HIDEOUS STRENGTH

Sex and love are supposed to go together, integrated as one whole, one entity. Sex concerns the physical, erotic side of love. Sex is also about love that is tender and giving, that makes me long to give all I have and am to someone. Each is good, even when considered alone. Together they have the strength of steel and the sparkle of diamonds.

As a result of the Fall, however, men and women experience love and sex separately. Nevertheless, love and sex are meant to be married to each other. Many of us who are married hang on to one of them, not caring so much about the other. Others of us hope that someday the two – the physical and emotional sides – will be reconciled.

A common pattern in marriage is for a man to be preoccupied with his sex drive while his wife feels starved of affection. But the two, affection and sex, are meant to be one, to be so much a part of one another as to be indistinguishable.

Marriage: Doorway to Freedom

Let me talk about marriage. I still believe marriage – the conventional notion of it – is one (not the only) high road to true freedom, whether we are talking about personal freedom or sexual freedom. In saying that, I certainly do not imply there is freedom only for the married. I am trying to avoid worldly cynicism about both marriage and singleness. Chastity is difficult – some would say impossible. Marriage can look like a trap. Lured by sex and/or affection, we crawl into the trap like lobsters after bait. How then can I speak of the freeing nature of marriage?

It is a freedom and beauty which married people uniquely may experience. I shall deal with marriage only incidentally and then only with the uniting of sex and love. Yet I must dismiss at once the notion that marriage is limiting. Or if it is, it is so only in the way prison gates are limiting when you are leaving the prison. You might have to squeeze through the prison doors to get out, but once out you are free. And the prison I am talking about, please remember, is not the prison of singleness, but the prison of wrong thinking about both marriage and singleness.

Freedom (at least the Greek idea of it) is doing what you were designed to do. Human beings have bodies and hearts designed for marriage and adaptable to singleness. There is freedom to be found, true freedom, in either.

Both marriage and singleness should be what the ocean is to a fish, what the sky is to a bird, what powdery snow is to an expert skier. They are rarely so conceived. The freedom of the slopes awaits the skier – but only the expert and experienced skier. First must come discipline, the discipline of learning how to stand, how to move and how to stop moving, how to cooperate with slope and surface, how to overcome fear, how to recognise and handle danger. Only then does true freedom yield its wonders. Until that point the skier's freedom is limited.

Inexperience and incompetence may themselves cause serious injury. If you recover from the injury, one of several things may happen. You may give up and never find out what real skiing freedom is, or you may continue but never gain confidence. However, if your commitment to skiing is wholehearted and deep, having learned a valuable lesson you may continue pursuing a high road to freedom.

The same is certainly true both of marriage and singleness. Their skills must be learned, and the learning may bring painful injuries. But let me, for a moment, focus on marriage.

We come to marriage not only untrained but damaged and largely unsanctified. 'Lifeless exteriors' need to be stripped off and painful injuries healed. Some of us are damaged emotionally, especially sexually, and it is this sort of damage I address in this book.

Learning Freedom on Your Own

In some of her conferences Leanne Payne talks about 'bent' men and women: those who, particularly within marriage, are bent toward their partners rather than reaching upward toward God. They are men and women who depend upon their partners for their fulfilment. We bring fulfilment in Christ *to* marriage. We do not look to marriage for a fulfilment that can only come from him. Single men and women who feel incomplete outside marriage because of their affectional and sexual needs are certain to be frustrated within marriage as well.

If we define *healing* (emotional) as a degree of restoration to what God intended us to be at creation, then healing and sanctification become synonymous, and healing becomes a part of wholeness. We should not look to marriage for sanctification except in the painful sense Mason talks about. We are continuously to be bringing sanctification *to* marriage. When each leans on Christ rather than on the other, each brings strength to the partnership. Structures with mutually leaning parts are unstable, liable to collapse.

Marriage should reflect the oneness of the Trinity. Such is God's intention for it. As Father, Son and Spirit are one, so are we to be. In our case the oneness is the oneness each of us should enjoy with God.

My focus is not on marriage itself. Rather, I am to be concerned about my own maturity within the marriage, about *my* sin and immaturity, not that of my spouse. The focus in many books about marriage is on how to have a good marriage. Our marriages improve greatly when we get past being 'bent' (mutually leaning) men and women and become God-leaning instead. To be so has greater importance than anything else in life, for both singles and marrieds.

God does not call married men and women to perfect marriages. He calls them to godliness within marriage. He calls singles to godliness as singles. It is every bit as tough to be godly in either state, each having their peculiarly sanctifying aspects. Godliness is about being set free, free as a single person or as a married person. In married people, godliness may not advance at the same rate in both spouses. Even so, my prime business is to obey God, whatever effect this may have on my marriage. To put the marriage before personal obedience is idolatry. Marital counselling can be helpful, but once the marriage is made central, Christ ceases to be central. As each partner makes Christ central, the marriage advances.

The Nature of Sexual Love

For each spouse individually, when affection and *eros* come together, lessons are learned as to what true love is all about. Sexual love is bodily love, love we learn through our bodies. We are bodily creatures, and God teaches us through our bodies.

Agape is the word the New Testament uses when it talks about the love of God. It is the love we Christians are supposed to have for God and our fellows. There is a feeling among Christians that *agape* must not be mentioned in the same breath as *eros* – bodily, physical love. Sexual love, we feel, is infinitely lower than *agape*. It is seen as inferior – as somewhat gross, unspiritual. But as C.S. Lewis points out, in the matter of the varieties of love, 'The highest does not stand without the lowest.'[1]

A major component in our problem is that we do not feel at home in our bodies. It is almost as though we don't live in them, as though we are off somewhere in a world of thought, or that we would be if we were not constantly reminded of our bodies by their hungers, their smells, the never ceasing growth of hair on them. So we bathe them, shave them, powder them, perfume and clothe them, all with the object of making them fit for the exalted world we inhabit. To such hygienic practices I have no objection. It is the motive behind it all that I suspect.

I suppose there is a sense in which bodily, sexual love, while not being an inferior form of love, is a lower love. It is lower in the sense of being more elementary, more basic, just as learning the alphabet is basic to learning to read, or learning to recognise and reproduce sounds is a prelude to learning to talk. To learn bodily love is to learn the basics of a more difficult lesson, the lesson of *agape* love. We must never despise or look down on our bodies. They are divine instruments.

Do I imply that only married people have a shot at learning *agape* love? I don't intend to. Marriage is one way to learn it, but some of the greatest God-lovers of all time have been single people, so marriage cannot be the only way. What I do say is that *agape* love for a spouse cannot be truly learned unless we learn to 'love and to cherish' our own bodies.

Ephesians 5:28–29 tell us, 'In this same way, husbands ought to love their wives as their own bodies. He who loves his wife loves himself. After all, no-one ever hated his own body, but he feeds and cares for it, just as Christ does the church.'

To enter a true experience of sexual love is to be on a high road to learning *agape* love.

Curiously, celibate mystics speak of divine love in sexual terms. Groping for language in which to describe what they experience of God's love, they are forced to use the language of the Song of Solomon. Contrary to the belief of some psycho-analytic writers, this is not because they are sexually frustrated. Far from frustrated, most of them are profoundly fulfilled. They experience love, ultimate love, that higher love of which sexual love is a symbol and a picture. Human language lacks the words to describe what they experience, the nearest being the language of the love that can exist between a man and a woman.

The Breadth of Sexual Love

Of course we must not limit our understanding of sexual love to the erotic sensations that accompany *making* love. Sexual love is deeper and broader than brief ecstasy. For a woman it includes gestation – the nine-month saga of the growth of a new life inside her body, that amazing poem of leisurely but profound changes. Her body both sings and groans – a singing and a groaning that are sexual in nature.

Nor is a man's sexual love mere orgasmic ecstasy. When a man feels tiny baby fingers curling around his own little finger, the sensations of wonder and affection as well as the urge to care for and protect arise out of sexual love. It is no longer erotic arousal, and it is certainly not the lust of a child molester. Rather, it is that which erotic arousal has led to: the joy of what is happening to him in that moment, the experience of a tiny replica of his own hand grasping his finger. Flesh that came from him now clings to him. The ecstasy at the beginning was a part of the greater whole.

In the same way, when a grandmother examines the photographs of her grandchildren and glows with pride and wonder at the second-generation fruit of her own body, it is sexual love she is experiencing. *Sexual love includes all that arises out of sex* – and grandchildren certainly do! We must not narrow sexual love down to what happens in bed or in a hayloft. It is a deep and broad God-given thing which covers a wide range of in-the-body experiences.

Sexual love is family love. It is the dependent and utterly selfish need-love of the child for its mother. In marriage it embraces friendship, a love necessary to every married couple. Friendship is first learned not outside the home, but among siblings in a family. It is also developed between parents and children as the children mature. Our habit of limiting the term *sexual* to erotogenic sensations is a master stroke of Satan, played out through idiocies of advertising. For it is Satan's design to split eroticism off from the totality of bodily love. And when he has achieved that, he weaves sexual chains around us.

C.S. Lewis writes about those particular chains both in his children's and in one of his adult fantasies, when he describes those pleasures which never satisfy but serve only to create a craving for more. Pleasures that come in the line of obedience to God do not leave us with craving, even though they may be repeated many times. We experience cravings, cravings for food that exceed our need for it and that ruin our health, cravings for sex that drive us insane with their endless demands and their failure truly to satisfy.

The Nature of Sexual Lust

Legitimate, God-given desire becomes lust the moment we make a god of it. To worship food is food lust. To be neurotic about getting our full quota of sleep becomes sleep lust. To be enslaved to erotic sensations represents sexual lust.

Lust never satisfies. One craves more and more while getting less and less out of it.

Sex can be a craving when love and sexual desire are split. It matters little what form the sexual activity takes – heterosexual sex within the marriage bond, or any other erotic delight. Ultimately, the craving leads to illicit or pathological forms of sex. The devil has achieved his aim. We fall into cravings that drive us into addiction to pornography, to masturbation, to excessive needs for sexual intercourse, heterosexual or homosexual, to child molestation and every form of perversion. Common to all of them is a hunger that can never be satisfied, that leaves us emptier than we were before.

Sexual love was never meant to be like that. When affection and fidelity blend with *eros*, true love flowers. Sexual activity then becomes an expression of love, not of need. Indeed the two (love and sex) seem one. Love expressed sexually under those conditions is always deeply satisfying. It does not leave an aching hunger, for it was designed to satisfy, not to torture. Nor does it enslave.

There is something more. Our enjoyment of the real thing is enhanced once the 'bad-magic' sex is abandoned.

Perverted sex is always diabolical. As long as we crave it we are unable to relish the real thing. It needs the power of Christ to break the enchantment and restore what is lost.

In everyday experience, the divorce between eroticism and affection takes one of two forms:

sometimes a yearning for erotic sensation is para-
mount, sometimes a craving for tenderness and
love. Using someone else's body to relieve oneself
represents love in the partner who gives, not in
the partner who takes. It is good as far as it goes.
It can be a stage in learning to love. But it can
also be a stage in deepening the divorce between
love and sex. Eventually things will go one way or
the other.

Lust had never satisfied me. An orgasm would
leave me wanting more, whether I could have it
or not. I have said elsewhere that the devil's
sadistic joke is to cause us to need more and
more stimulation for less satisfaction in return.
For sex and love, *eros* and *agape*, were meant
to be welded and wedded. And to the degree
that they are, *making* love becomes infinitely
more satisfying. *A wrong attitude to our bodies
renders impossible that welding and wedding of*
eros and agape.

Respect for the Body

How do we feel about our bodies – hatred? God
desires to inculcate *respect* – not fear – respect and
honour for him, and respect and honour (even joy)
for what he created. He wishes us to be thankful
for our bodies, which are a gift from him. The
sexual parts of us demand 'greater honour' and
also to be treated with modesty because they
are less presentable publicly (1 Cor 12:23). We
should all be profoundly grateful for our sexual
parts, and *should express that gratitude in worship and praise*.

Fear of the body? Everything created by God,
including our bodies, is good, and according to

Paul it is to be received with thanksgiving, being sanctified by the word of God and prayer (1 Tim 4:1–5). And while exhibitionism and immodesty are inappropriate and sinful, a natural awareness of and enjoyment of one's body and all its parts, and a wholehearted rejoicing in God's creation of, sanctification of and indwelling of it is important. 'After all,' writes Paul, 'no-one ever hated his own body, but he feeds and cares for it, just as Christ does the church' (Eph 5:29).

Why should some of us fear our bodies? On the surface it is because we associate many of their sensations with erotic sex, and that our sex urges are almost uncontrollable. If this is the case, it becomes easy to feel that erotic feelings are in themselves evil (except when in marriage we are actually engaged in sexual intercourse – and sometimes even then).

There is indeed hope. The person who fears, John tells us, 'is not made perfect in love.' Indeed, 'perfect love drives out fear' (1 Jn 4:18).

Many other men and women I know have overcome their fears in relation to sex after what has been called prayer healing or inner healing. Because inner healing is controversial and widely misunderstood I want to deal with it more fully later.

Not Respecting One's Body

Other people have no such fears. They are much less inhibited about displaying their nakedness, especially in sexual settings. In Spanish there is an expression of contempt: *sin verguenza*. Literally meaning 'without shame,' it does not refer to the experience our forefathers had before the Fall

when they were 'naked but unashamed.' Rather
it refers to the shamelessness of persons who
laugh because they can make others blush by
flaunting their sins. It is to glory in one's sin,
to be proud of one's sin. Such people cheapen
sexuality and do not respect the bodies God gave
them.

It is the very opposite of that for which God
made us in his own image. For the present all
I wish to point out is the way in which love and
sex can become divorced. They are meant to be
together. The giving and receiving of love can
and should be fully expressed and deeply felt in
'lovemaking.'

Should they be divorced in your own case, take
heart. It is the will of God that they come together
again. I cannot say that my solution will be yours,
and in any case we will get to solutions in due
course. But be assured of two things. First, there
is a depth to the love that expresses itself in sexual
coupling which a focus on orgasms misses entirely.
And second, God plans that depth for you. It is
your heritage in Christ, and he waits to give
it to you.

Sex and the Castaway

Sex is not intended only for procreation but also,
and more importantly, for communication.

I define masturbation as *bodily manipulation in
pursuit of an orgasm*.[2] I first wrote on masturbation in *Eros Defiled*, and although by the time I
wrote at some length on it in *Eros Redeemed* my
ideas were clearer, nonetheless the chapters in
both books are well worth reading. In *Eros Defiled*
I compared masturbation with the experience of

a castaway on a desert island. Isolation of that kind breeds a yearning, a craving for the sound of a human voice, for the companionship of other human beings. I have always maintained that masturbation is an undesirable anomaly since sex is meant, among other things, to be interpersonal communion. Sexual union has also been seen down the centuries as an anticipation of the loving intimacy that will one day exist between God and his people.

The Significance of Shame

What started me thinking again about masturbation was the amount of shame it still causes today. We are not ashamed about sex in marriage; we can even talk about it in social gatherings. Healthy people are not ashamed of being naked under appropriate circumstances. I have known enough of the pain and the shame of my own masturbating to have compassion for someone who struggles in the Valley of Humiliation. But the modern tendency is different. Opinions have changed. Many young people nowadays masturbate freely – but discreetly. And millions of older and married people do the same. It is something most married people prefer not to think about.

I have already rejected the view that masturbation is a normal release of sexual tension. Yet is it true that masturbators experience no shame? I question it, though certainly people nowadays have a much easier time suppressing shame than people of my age did. But is not shame one key to understanding sexual issues? Paul seems to think so (1 Cor 11:6).

I believe the shame is still there, suppressed or not, hidden under pseudosophistication. And if I am right, surely the fact is significant. If you have shame *about something you have been taught is normal*, then 'nature itself' is trying to teach you something. And when I say that 'nature itself' tries to teach you, I am talking about primary shame, as opposed to cultural shame.

I have compassion for the victims of masturbation, but the time has now come for me to challenge the views that prevail and to call on Christians to face reality. Masturbation is sin. It is not *grave* sin, not nearly as serious as pride, or cruelty, or even unkindness. But still it is sin.

A Wrong Attitude to Masturbation

Let me state my reasons for calling it sin at all. It is sin because sexuality was not given us for that purpose. In masturbating we use our bodily parts for a purpose God never intended for them.

My first argument, then, for calling masturbation sin is what could be called the *argument of design*. My body is mine only in the sense that I am responsible for its proper use. I am its steward. For what was my body designed? The Westminster Confession asks a similar if not identical question. 'What is the chief end of man?' The answer the authors give is, 'Man's chief end is to glorify God and to enjoy him forever.'

Paul expresses the same end for our bodies. He concludes, 'So glorify God in your body' (1 Cor 6:20 RSV). The argument I have been using from chapter three onward concerns the offering of our bodies to God as an act of worship. In the NIV version of Romans 6, Paul even mentions the *parts* of our bodies, saying, 'Do not offer the parts of your body to sin, as instruments of wickedness . . . offer the parts of your body to him [God] as instruments of righteousness. For sin shall not be your master' (Rom 6:13–14).

My body was not designed to masturbate. My body was designed to be used exclusively to glorify God. To use it in any other way is to rob God of something that is his by right, for there are no morally neutral actions.

You say: So everything becomes black and white. Are there no shades of grey? Yes, plenty of them. But even the whitest shade of grey has some black in it. So if you should go on to say, 'Well, it really doesn't matter that much, does it?' then I must insist that sin always matters. Our sin brought about the death of Christ.

Just as speech was given to us in order that we might communicate truths rather than lies or gossip, so the sexual parts of our bodies were designed to copulate. Remember, copulation is far more than orgasmic experiences. It was to be a sharing, a sort of gateway to deeper sharing, a never-ending mutual revelation of the depths of our souls. Yet copulation can be entirely selfish, a mere using of somebody's body to gratify myself, which is little different from masturbation.

My second argument for calling masturbation sin – closely related to the first argument – is that masturbation is *a form of idolatry*. Our bodies are to be offered to God. Again, I know that married lovemaking can itself be a selfish pursuit of bodily sensation. But I repeat: it was

not designed to be. At that point it becomes
lust.

Yet I know how some men and women struggle.
How bitter some people feel in their vain struggle
against it! Younger people, young marrieds away
from their spouses, have a particularly difficult
time. I know a man whose problem *began* with
marriage. Like all sin, masturbation must be dealt
with compassionately and in love.

Masturbation is to make a god of my bodily
sensations, and there is but one God. To make a
god of my sensations is to become an idolater.

The Psychological Damage

Classical behavioural psychology tells us that
pleasure, even more than pain, shapes behaviour
in all life forms. We learn without realizing we are
learning. When you do something and it gives you
pleasure, you are more likely to do it again. Even
worms learn (in time) to avoid certain surfaces.
More intelligent life forms learn faster. Especially
children. Buy a child ice cream, and the child will
want it every time you pass the store. The pleasure
of the ice cream has 'stamped in' ice cream-eating
behaviour.

If a young, unmarried woman masturbates with
pleasurable fantasies of another woman's body,
the immediate effect of the masturbation will be
a sort of relief, an easing of any sexual tension.
The long-term effect will be that the pleasure
of the experience will increase her proclivity to
homosexuality in real life.

Or when a married man masturbates contemplating in his mind the body of a woman with
whom he once had an affair, he 'stamps in' three

things: first, the tendency to repeat the performance – to the detriment of his relationship with his wife; second, and at first perhaps only slightly, the possibility of seeking the woman out in real life and having an affair with her, or of seducing someone else; and third, the increasing tendency to be self-absorbed in any sexual relationship.

Sex is communication, communication with real persons. No communication takes place with a fantasy, and none takes place when you are merely focusing on your own body.

Unreality

The real danger is always the danger of coming under the control of dark powers, just as in any form of misuse of our sexuality. Masturbation certainly tends to be compulsive. One of Satan's goals is to lead us into an unreal world. And one of the signs that I am in unreality, under Satan's control, is that God's power in my life can be deflected by sin.

In my case the habit was certainly compulsive. I was *not* in control, could not quit entirely. I had lost that freedom wherewith Christ had made me free – until he rescued me. In my case, and many years ago, a personal word from the Lord changed matters. One night as I lay reflecting, he drew near and told me the practice grieved him, and that he wished me to quit. With the word of the Lord came the power of the Lord, and I was set free from a bondage I alone could never have broken. But such is not everyone's experience. Later, I deliberately sinned again, and though I still had some control, for a number of years I continued to struggle. My freedom now is too valuable ever to lose again.

Unreality is the master stroke of the Deceiver. It produced our blindness to our sins and our tendency to hide from God and one another. It produces psychological denial, defensiveness in the face of criticism and suppression of our shame. To live in it is a habit, the habit of choosing unreality. Instead, remembering in whose presence we live, we should think every thought, speak every word, perform every action before God. (And I believe few of us would be so abandoned as to masturbate in his presence.)

Victims are not free. We were redeemed that we might no longer be under the dominion of darkness but might be really free. And only God's Son can restore our freedom. Freedom is something positive. It is not merely freedom *from* but freedom *to* something. We are freed from slavery in order that we might live to and for Christ. Freedom is being what we were designed to be, doing what we were designed to do. We were not designed to be a race of masturbators. Which we are.

'It's Impossible Not To'

Now for the brighter side. Nothing is impossible with God. For married and for single folk, for pubescent youngsters and for dirty old men and women, the norm is, actually, *not* to masturbate. Freedom under God is what he created us for, and freedom in Christ is what the Son died to restore to us.

We must realise, of course, that God has his own priorities, his own order for sorting us out and making us holy. The thing that may humiliate us the most is not necessarily what God wants to deal with in us first. God desires to free you from your ambivalence – the many contradictory desires which pull you this way and that. It is possible for you to be freed, but ambivalence will have to go first.

If you masturbate regularly and then you stop, nothing dreadful will happen. The fear that something will burst is simply not true. No boiler will rupture and no kettle inside you explode. Rather, your experience will be like that of a mechanical toy when it is fully wound. You will be fully ready to perform sexually, but the tension in your 'spring' will not affect your inner rest, because the spring is locked in that state. In the same way, a married person does not have to have sex even when gloriously aroused. The arousal can be allowed to subside. Interpersonal relationships are impossible, in fact, if both partners insist on getting all they think they need right away.

Can God deliver you? Of course he can. If he isn't doing so at the moment, he may, incredible though it may seem to you, have a prior concern with something else in your life. While I remain firm in my conviction that masturbation has to go, I recognise that God has his own order in dealing with sin. Sin is always serious. But when an injured man comes into the hospital, his injuries must be dealt with one at a time. By all means ask God to help you, but do not focus too much on this one thing. Focus on positive virtues like loving your neighbour as yourself. Or if you focus on sin, think of someone you may have hurt this week – by your sarcasm, your coldness, your forgetfulness, your laziness, your lack of tact and courtesy. Then confess these and set them right.

Again, thank God for all your sexual feelings. Don't hate them. They may be as difficult to manage as a canoe in the rapids, but they represent one of God's richest gifts to you. He made you to feel sexual desire. Be glad and rejoice in it. Thank him, too, for the day when you will be master of your sexual drives. Though it tarry, it will come, if you let God be master in other areas in your life.

Do you despise yourself? You can quit doing that right now. Refuse to listen to the torturous accusations of the accuser of the brethren, who accuses you day and night (Rev 12:10). If you are cast down, God waits for you with arms wide open. By all means groan, but take your shame to the throne of grace where the blood will wash it away. Your will is being freed. And it will be freed from the grip of masturbation too, one day. So learn to laugh at your chains, in faith. Thomas R. Kelly says, 'Humility does not rest ... upon bafflement and discouragement and self-disgust at our shabby lives, a brow-beaten, dog-slinking attitude. It rests upon the disclosure of the consummate wonder of God.'[3] He also says, 'When you catch yourself again, lose no time in self-recriminations, but breathe a silent prayer for forgiveness and begin again, just where you are. Offer this broken worship up to Him and say: "This is what I am except Thou aid me." Admit no discouragement, but ever return quietly to Him and wait in His Presence.'[4]

We are nothing apart from his help. He knows it. We know it. To admit what we are (for instance, to say, 'Among other things, I masturbate – and it's wrong') is to begin to walk with God. Honesty with ourselves, with God and at times with one another will be a step toward health and spiritual growth.

Chapter 6

Sex and Gender Confusion

*The earthquake that is shaking men and women,
their roles and interrelationships, is part and parcel
of the world culture's tectonic plates. The changes in
our gender roles are only one aspect of the upheaval
that accompanies the death of one epoch and the
birth of another.*
SAM KEEN, FIRE IN THE BELLY

Sex and gender are not the same. Our *sexual*
identity has to do with our being *male* or
female, man or woman, boy or girl. Our sex is
determined by the shape of our bodies and their
organs, by our hormones and the brain centres
that control them. It is physical in nature, rooted
in our biology.

Our *gender* identity has to do with something
slightly different – our sense of being manly or
womanly. *Masculine* and *feminine* have to do with
character, and disposition, and above all with
our feelings about ourselves as men or women.
Obviously sex and gender are to some extent
dependent on the other. But the wide variety
of characteristics in both men and women would
suggest that the correlation is not exact.

Psychoanalyst Karl Stern tells us in *The Flight
from Woman* that 'Man in his fullness is bisex-
ual.'[1] By this he means that every man (and

every woman also) contains both masculinity and femininity.

Manliness and Womanliness

So what is – not the female – but the feminine? The traditional view is that God, the source of both masculinity and femininity, is more masculine than the most masculine male. What does this mean? How can God, who clearly is the source of the feminine as well as the masculine, be *more* masculine than male human beings?

A key difference, noted by C.S. Lewis, is that the male is the initiator and the female the responder. In this sense God acts in a male way toward his world and his people. It is in this sense that God, who is neither male nor female, is more masculine than the most masculine male. God speaks, and *ex nihilo* the universe is initiated into being. He takes initiative with every human being – in creating us, speaking to us, sending his Son for us. His masculinity is expressed in this way. He is basically not one who reacts, but who *acts*.

Thus when any of us (male or female) responds to God's initiative, our response is essentially feminine in nature. In any divine-human encounter, *God always takes the initiative, and we humans respond* – either with faith and trust or else with rebellion.

Appearances can be misleading. It may appear at times that we take matters into our own hands, taking the initiative ourselves. But it is never so. When David cries out in distress to God (in Ps 38, for example), he does so for two reasons. First, God has taken the initiative to implant a hunger for himself in David. Second, God has already given David a lot of training in hopeless situations, precisely so that David might learn to cry out. Once again, God initiates. *David's psalms are responses to circumstances into which God has brought him.*

Prayer is prayer only when it is a response to what God is doing in us. God is always and supremely the initiator. We are all responders, women usually having a greater gift for responsiveness and sensitivity than men. These qualities, rather than lace, frills and perfume, lie at the root of what we call femininity.

In addition, both men and women bear some of God's nurturing qualities – women usually more than men. Women bear children from their own bodies, feeding them with milk manufactured in their own breasts. So it is understandable that most women show more patience with children, greater tolerance of their ceaseless activity and noise, more compassion. When men show these qualities, they respond to the feminine in themselves. When women fail to show it, their femininity is not yet fully developed.

Men and women alike are thus gifted. Yet just as women are more gifted with gifts of femininity than men, so men are more given to initiating. We live in a day of profound confusion about such issues, as both men and women search for answers, men especially searching for their true identity.[2]

We sometimes say, 'Jim's real man,' or 'Bettina's all woman.' We imply degrees of proximity to manliness and womanliness. Some people never think about such questions because they have buried their fears in their unconscious minds, but there are men who secretly wish they were more like other men, while some women wish that they had the same interests and instincts they see in other women.

The implication that arises from the statement 'Bettina's all woman' must be examined. Is there an ideal for womanliness and manliness, and if so, what is it in each case? *To whom do we look for a model?* Stereotypes of both men and women break down when we examine them.

The woman of Proverbs 31 is nothing to despise as a model for womanhood. Feminists might argue that she is depicted as her husband's slave. He enjoys the privilege of power – 'sits in the gate' (is one of the city's leaders) while she by her slavish devotion to him and his household keeps him there. On the other hand, women who have an excessive need to be submissive and to devote themselves to their husband's pleasure and success will feel uncomfortable with her independent ways. This paragon of a woman teaches, organises her household, handles money independently and makes successful forays into the 'male' world of business and finance. We need to revise our notions of the biblical picture of ideal womanhood.

In every culture there is an ideal form of manliness and womanliness. 'Be strong, Philistines! Be men, or you will be subject to the Hebrews, as they have been to you. Be men, and fight!' the Philistines were told, as they faced Israel on one occasion (1 Sam 4:9). The Philistines clearly had their own point of view about manliness.

But so has the apostle Paul. In 1 Corinthians 16:13 we find him echoing the words of the Philistines. 'Be on your guard; stand firm in the faith; be men of courage; be strong.' For Paul, masculinity and therefore the greatest element in manliness means strength in the face of opposition and persecution.

For men, Jesus is the model of manliness. We are presented by Western society with such models as the jock, the wimp, the womaniser and Rambo. Jesus was none of these, yet if there is to be found an ideal of true manliness anywhere, then we must look to the portrait of him as it is found in the Gospels. I shall do that later. For now, it is enough to make one comment about Jesus – that we rarely think of him in terms of his maleness and his masculinity. If the question is raised, we feel that we must say, 'Yes, of course. Jesus is most certainly a manly man.' Yet Jesus – at least the distorted image of him that comes through preaching and storytelling – does not conform to our confused idea of what a manly man should look like.

We must, therefore, use words like *manly* and *womanly* more carefully. After all, there are clear biblical models of manliness and womanliness.

Gender, then, is not the same as sex. God and the angelic hosts have gender. They do not have sex.

But, so what? Are not men to be masculine and women feminine? Well, not exactly. I do not know all that happened when God drew a rib out of the first man and from it formed woman. The account is so brief that innumerable fanciful but contradictory theories exist about it, all supposedly based on the words of the text. It may be that what I am about to say is equally fanciful, but at least it may help us to understand the distinction between sex and gender.

The Prototype Human

I like to think of Adam before the mysterious
operation not as the prototype *male* human, but
simply as the prototype *human being*. I am told
that there is support in the Hebrew text for the
idea. I also like to think that when the operation
took place, most of the feminine qualities but
also some of the masculine qualities were used
to form the woman, and that some of the feminine qualities but most of the masculine qualities
remained. After all, how could men and women
relate to one another, unless each were to contain
within their inner selves something of the other's
nature? How else would mutual understanding be
possible? Men and women both experience 'mixed
gender' characteristics, even though men are male
and women are female.

Women who say, 'I can't understand men,' are
denying the masculinity in their own beings. Men
who say, 'Women make no sense at all to me,' deny
that which is feminine in themselves, and in so
doing deny their God-given capacity to understand
women. Both men and women of that sort are
really less than complete men and women.

After all the (prototype) man was made in the
image and likeness of God. And in God's person,
and from his being, come all the properties we call
masculine and feminine. We think of masculinity
in terms of initiative and strength, qualities God
supremely displays. We have already seen that he
takes the initiative sovereignly and always. His
strength is infinite.

On the other hand we think of sensitivity,
nurturing and responsiveness as feminine qualities. God has feminine qualities too. He tells the

inhabitants of Jerusalem, 'As a mother comforts her child, so will I comfort you' (Is 66:13). Moses describes God's reactions to Israel as follows: 'like an eagle that stirs up its nest and hovers over its young, that spreads its wings to catch them and carries them on its pinions. The LORD alone led him [Israel]' (Deut 32:11–12). The perfect God displayed the feminine qualities of a mother eagle.

In deep distress Jesus once cried out, 'O Jerusalem, Jerusalem, you who kill the prophets and stone those sent to you, how often I have longed to gather your children together, as a hen gathers her chicks under her wings' (Lk 13:34). The perfect man expresses the 'feminine' feelings of a mother hen.

We may take it then that God's ideal for manhood includes qualities we call feminine. If, for example, sensitivity is not a male quality, where do male artists, poets and musicians get their sensitivity from? Are they less men than professional football players or men who drive trucks, drink beer and wear cowboy boots? Some might say yes. Or is it simply that male artists have made more use of the feminine side of their natures? Are some men perhaps afraid – afraid because of cultural stereotypes of manliness we have created, of their feminine traits?

Similarly, is there something wrong with drive and initiative in a woman? Remember, the Proverbs 31 woman displays both of these 'masculine' qualities. 'She considers a field and buys it; out of her earnings she plants a vineyard. She sets about her work vigorously; her arms are strong for her tasks. She sees that her trading is profitable . . . She makes linen garments and sells them, and supplies the merchants with sashes. She is

clothed with strength and dignity; she can laugh
at the days to come' (Prov 31:16–18, 24–25).

Let it be established then that males major in
qualities we call masculine, and minor in qualities we call feminine, and that females major in
the feminine and minor in the masculine. Men
should not be afraid of the feminine side of their
natures, nor women of their masculine traits. Our
natures will be unbalanced and incomplete if we
are, for men without feminine traits *are not yet
fully men*, and women with no masculine side to
them are *lacking in the full development of their
womanhood*.

In Search of a Real Man

I say masculinity is male, meaning it is meant
to be more male than female. Men are currently
disheartened and confused. Feminist reactions to
male violence, to male irresponsibility, to male
shiftlessness and to male exploitation of women
are all rooted in justice, even though the underlying feminist philosophy is, I believe, neither valid
nor godly. In the face of women's understandable
protests and the male bashing of feminist-oriented
literature (which currently greatly exceeds literature about how to be helpful to men), men are
uncertain what they are supposed to be.

Jesus: Model of Manliness

Jesus practised what he preached. But what did
he practise in relation to his authority? How did
he exercise his authority on earth? The question
has great importance. For as he is in relation to
us, so we all must be in relation to others, and so

we men must be in relation to women. So, also, church leaders must be in relation to members of the congregation. In this chapter, primarily for men, I will look at how Jesus provided a model of manhood, considering especially the last days of his life.

Though he was both divine and human, the impression one gets from reading the Gospels is that Jesus operated primarily in his humanity on earth. While in his atoning death it was essential that he be God *and* man, in most of his earthly acts he seems to act *as man empowered by the Spirit of God*. That is why Paul refers to him as the second man or last Adam (1 Cor 15:45, 47). The fact is of incalculable importance. It means he performed his miracles, gave his teaching, not as God, but *as a human being filled with the Spirit*. He did not cease to be God, but his *mode* was human. How else was he tempted? You can't tempt God. Why else did he need to be anointed and filled with the Holy Spirit? *You don't fill God with the Spirit*!

Please understand what I am saying. I am *not* asserting that his divinity played no part in our redemption. We needed a Saviour who was and is fully God and fully man.[3] I stress the fullness of his human experience because it is the one less taken into account. We can do the same works he did only if he did them not as God, but as man. We cannot and must not play God, but we can follow Jesus and walk in his Spirit. But it is of his maleness that I most want to speak.

Where Adam failed both morally and as a man, Jesus did not. In his triumph he opens the way to true manhood and true womanhood. At the heart of the human nature of Christ lies what is in God's own heart. For he is God the Son. Servanthood lies at the heart of his relationship with others, and servanthood is seen supremely in his redeeming death. As he said, 'Whoever wants to be first must be your slave – just as the Son of Man did not come to be served, but to serve, and to give his life as a ransom for many' (Mt 20:27–28).

True servanthood is not wimping out. It includes speaking frankly, honestly and openly, yet not in petulant anger or needless truculence. Jesus loved the very people who roused his anger. Why else would he eat with Pharisees, for example?

Jesus displayed manliness in standing up to Pharisees, Sadducees and teachers of the law. He was in no way cowed by their learning or their pseudoauthority. Some of the passages in John 8 and in Matthew 23 make John the Baptist's outburst sound mild. Yet while Jesus was enraged at their abuse of power, he still loved the Pharisees, as he loved the Jewish nation in entirety. He would hardly have eaten with them had he hated them. In his manhood he can show both stern anger and tenderness. He moves from Matthew 23:33 ('You snakes! You brood of vipers! How will you escape being condemned to hell?') to Matthew 23:37 ('O Jerusalem . . . I have longed to gather your children together, as a hen gathers her chicks').

The Last Adam, a True Man

Throughout his life Jesus displayed the capacity to initiate, to lead in new ways that bucked the whole society. He was fearless in his initiating. While he used the rabbinical teaching method, his disciples were men who had been trained in the hurly-burly of life. They would hardly be the training material preferred by most rabbis. Because he always spoke the truth, even when it hurt, many of his disciples took offence and left him (Jn 6:66).

Many men prefer the company of other men because they feel uncomfortable when exposed for too long to the company of women and children. Jesus loved children and rebuked his disciples for attempting to hinder their access to him. His love and his sense of responsibility also caused him to seek out and to stand up for the poor and the oppressed. He had the capacity to stick with anything he was called by God to do, whatever the consequences might be and however great the cost to him.

As for his feminine side, it may be less obvious, but I have already cited Christ's use of the picture of a hen gathering her brood under her wings. There are also examples of his capacity to feel and display tenderness. At the grave of Lazarus, he wept for the hopelessness experienced by those who did not believe, their hopelessness before the Grim Reaper.

A yet more moving example is seen at the crucifixion. In great pain and in a physical state of shock, Jesus is still able to think of the needs of others. (Women are better at bearing pain and still caring for dependants than men are. The trait is a feminine trait. A mother needs it.) Agonised though he is on the cross, Jesus still has his mother's needs on his heart. He knows John will look after her more conscientiously than his own brothers will. So he calls first to his mother, then to John, 'Woman, behold your son . . . [son], behold your mother' (Jn 19:26–27 NKJV). Feminine traits are not wimpish traits. It takes enormous strength to take action in the

life of another when your body is screaming its
protests.

But, *does a real man ever show weakness*? Does a
real man turn to friends and tell them he's reached
his limit? Does he say, 'Please stick around, guys.
I really need your support right now. I'm not sure
if I can take what's coming to me'? Is that not
a sign of unmanly weakness? For some it may
be, but not for Jesus. He shared his own need
for human contact – with men with whom he
shared his heart. Right before he was arrested
and crucified, 'He took Peter and the two sons
of Zebedee along with him, and he began to be
sorrowful and troubled. Then he said to them, "My
soul is overwhelmed with sorrow to the point of
death. Stay here and keep watch with me"' (Mt
26:37–38).

What was his need? It was that he knew what
was coming to him, the stark horror of that death
that was to be like no other human death. He
needed a time of prayer so that he could wrestle
through to peace in his soul. Yet if God was his
help, why the need also for male human beings?
Was God the Father not enough? The fact was that
the Father God seemed a long way away right then
to the man Jesus. What ought we to tell him? Keep
a stiff upper lip? 'Just have faith, Jesus!'

No. He needed Peter, James and John around,
because he was human. He was facing the most
horrendous test of his human experience, for he
was to suffer as a man. And as a man he craved
the physical proximity of those dear to him. He
was not ashamed to ask for it. Christ's maturity
as a man is seen throughout the Gospel story.
Read again of his arrest, flogging, vicious bullying,
trial and crucifixion. The victim was a manly man.

Weary, in shock, in pain, he was manly enough to keep his eyes on the goal. That was what mattered to him. *He despised what he went through, counting the prize well worth what he was enduring*.

So how do we get to be like him? So stunning is the manhood we see that we recognise at once the vast difference that separates us. And though he has 'made us nigh' by his atoning death, the difference in our respective characters is appalling. If this is manhood, do we have any hope of becoming men?

Well, there are ways in which we may become progressively more and more like him, especially as we gaze upon him. But we must not forget that the fears and shames we have buried in our unconscious minds will have to be exhumed. We buried them before they were dead. To have the Spirit dig them up again will involve fear, shame, pain. Only he can do it for us. He is sensitive, and when he probes, his fingers will be gentle. He will not make the process any more difficult than we can bear.

Gender Identity Confusion

Gender identity confusion, the final result of the Fall that I shall discuss, is the failure of my manhood or my womanhood to reach its full maturity. It is a *forme fruste* of my true being, the failure of my real self to flower. Sometimes (but not always) it may result in the consciousness that my body has one sex, but that my experience is not the same as secure members of my sex. But there are grades and degrees of the confusion. Only when it is very severe does it make heterosexual life intolerable. Moderate grades of it may raise the doubt in my

mind from time to time as to whether *there is
something wrong with me – perhaps I'm gay*. But
often there is not even that.

What then is gender identity confusion? We all
know to what *sex* we belong. The very form of our
bodies, the shape of our sexual apparatus makes
the matter clear. Men are men and women are
women. How could there be any confusion?

But gender confusion can foul up our sexuality
and the bodily mechanisms of sexual response. It
can mess up the way our bodies function. Confusion about our gender identity will affect our
bodily responses to members of our own and the
opposite sex and thus our relationships with both.
Normally we will be attracted to members of our
own sex for companionship and common interests,
and to the opposite sex for companionship and
also for romance and marriage. But where there
is confusion about our gender identity we may
be attracted physically to members of our own
sex instead of, or as well as, to members of the
opposite sex.

Men in Western cultures, middle-class men particularly, are lonely. We're afraid that to want or to
seek close companionship with a man might mean
we are gay. So we congregate as men, but rarely
do we deeply share the concerns of our hearts.
Women are better at it than men. With a dawning
men's movement, men are getting in touch with
other men once again.

Sexual identity confusion can be associated with
homosexual temptations, homosexual dreams and
preoccupation with the bodies and the genitals of
members of one's own sex, as well as with a flight
from the gender characteristics of one's own sex.
But it can be concerned with much more. Even

the excessive 'jockness' of jocks, the 'supermacho' qualities of some men can arise in this way. Leanne Payne tells us gender confusion lies behind the story of 'the husband who from time to time jumps in bed with other women in order to assure himself he is still a man . . . [or of] the young man who is guilt ridden over occasional sexual affairs, unable to commit himself to a woman, and now in clinical depression, contemplating suicide.'[4]

Inevitably sexual identity confusion and gender identity confusion go together.

We must, however, keep the shared nature of gender in mind constantly. And men say 'God is male', not only by their words, but by playing God in the home. Women who have been subject to suffocatingly authoritative fathers have told me repeatedly, 'I can pray to Jesus – but not to God the Father. I just can't.' God is not male, he is masculine, and also feminine.

As I minister to men and women with various sexual problems, I find again and again that underlying their problems is confusion about their gender identity. Addiction to pornography, the temptation to molest children, to exhibit oneself, to be a peeping Tom, to engage in animal sex, and the ongoing inability to quit masturbation – all can be associated with some degree of gender identity confusion. (I am also convinced that homophobia itself – the fear and hatred of homosexual persons – arises from the unconscious fear of being tarred with the same brush, which itself results from identity confusion.)

And though the victims may not realise it, identity confusion is also associated in married men and women with an inability to relate to their partners in the fullness of their maleness or

femaleness. They therefore derive less from their
marital experience than God intends for them, so
that they search for what is missing in sinful ways,
never finding what they seek.

Origins of the Confusion

To explain how sex and gender confusion arise I
must talk about our origins, about the relationship
between heredity and environment. Do we have
gender confusion because we were born with it?
Or because of what happened earlier in our experience? Is the confusion inherited or environmental
in origin? I suppose geneticists and environment-
alists will discuss the matter until doomsday. As
a Christian I have to bear both factors in mind.
The effects of the Fall come to me genetically.
The sins of my early life (certainly sins committed
against me) come environmentally. Therefore both
factors may play a part in determining my gender
confusion or lack of it.

We will have to look at this matter more carefully when we deal with the issue of homosexuality. It is there that the issue has assumed too
great a significance. All of us have a vulnerability
to particular sins. And our weaknesses differ. You
may be tempted to steal or to lie from time to
time, whereas my difficulty may be to perpetual
drunkenness or bitterness. Whatever the form of
the sin, heredity and environment will both play a
part. And neither of the two constitutes an excuse.
We are responsible for our sin.

Healing can be of help in greatly diminishing
the force of temptation. The difference can be like
night and day. Healing is merely a part of something greater and more important, our ongoing

sanctification. In fact, the less we talk about
healing and the more we think in terms of sanctification, the clearer we will be in our minds.

Whatever the term we use, buried memories of
incidents when we sinned and were sinned against
profoundly influence our behaviour. They make us
more vulnerable than we need be to temptation.

I have misgivings about some psychoanalytic
doctrines. But I am convinced that Sigmund
Freud's re-emphasis of the *unconscious* is of enormous importance. You have one. I have one. And
their contents influence our behaviour every day.

I call it *re-emphasis* because Freud's idea is a
biblical one. 'Who can discern his errors?' the
bewildered psalmist asks. 'Forgive my hidden
faults' (Ps 19:12). Jeremiah understands the problem more clearly still. 'The heart is deceitful above
all things and beyond cure,' he cries. 'Who can
understand it?' And God calls back to him, 'I the
Lord search the heart and examine the mind' (Jer
17:9–10).

Who can understand the heart? God can. He
knows the hidden depths of my heart, even secrets
I keep locked so deeply that I do not know them
myself, secrets I can no longer remember. I may
think I know myself well, know my character
accurately. But I am a fool if I think that. My
heart is a mass of hidden fears, lusts, hates and
passions.

Freud's explanation is that it is our fear – our
fear of the buried, hidden mess – that keeps
us from knowing. Such are the contents of the
unconscious that we dare not lift the lid to peer
within. Memories of early events we cannot bear
to think about, memories whose implications are
utterly unendurable to us, still lie hulking in the

dark shadows of our unconscious. And while the unconscious may still exert a powerful, unseen influence on our behaviour, only in our dreams do its contents slip out, and then only in disguise.

I can only suppose that the existence of an unconscious mind is also an effect of the Fall. It involves internal, mental deceit, an internal, mental covering up of a host of facts about ourselves and our personalities. It also covers from our awareness *sinful attitudes which grieve God* – attitudes which you would deny indignantly if I were to accuse you of them. Whole tracts of memory have been buried. They were buried furtively in the darkness, and we no longer know where to find them. What we know (or think we know) about ourselves is only the tip of the iceberg.

Pandora's Box

Freud was also right in suggesting that healing from conditions he called neuroses could follow our rediscovery of unconscious material. Healing *can* follow, but it rarely does. For we buried the memories not only in fear but also in sin and bitterness. Often we were sinned against. And as we shall see later, it is only as we pardon those who have sinned against us, entering into an understanding of God's forgiveness to us, that the cure takes place.

We say we have no fear of knowing the hidden contents of our unconscious minds. We say, 'If there's a hidden secret there, I want to know about it. After all, if it's causing problems, why should I be afraid of it?' But the child inside us, the child that once we were, has not ceased to be terrified. To approach the memory in reality is to become that child again, to know the same terror. So practised are we – from long-established habit – at avoiding the curtain-enshrouded entrance to the darkness, that we miss it every time we pass it, miss the cowering child that tries to hurry from it, but never can, trembling by the entrance. I have known people to scream in terror when God begins to pull the curtain back.

For now it is only necessary to know that our hearts are dark and deceitful, and that the hidden depths of our hearts contain the keys to things we do not understand about ourselves. But the symptoms I have described and the sins they give rise to can be painful. We tend to be very ashamed of sexual weaknesses. We hate to think of ourselves as kinky. No one wants to be a freak.

Yet all of us are freaks. None of us are what God intended us to be. But we must face what we are and begin right there. Sam Keen says, 'The chains that bind us most tightly are those we refuse to acknowledge.'

Thank God he will not leave us in this sad state of denial! He is faithful and true. He has plans for all of us.

Chapter 7

The Roots of Inversion

*Perhaps . . . demands from within the Church,
outrageous as they are, have done us all a favour.
They've pointed quite forcefully to the fact that the
Church as a whole has not known how to minister to
the healing these sufferers need.*
LEANNE PAYNE, THE BROKEN IMAGE

For both men and women, negative experiences with a member of the opposite sex range widely and can produce both hatred and an exaggerated need for conquest. Common to them all is the absence of that peace and quiet joy that should characterize an ongoing male–female relationship.

The most seriously disturbed reaction is the extreme homosexual experience of inversion, the underlying and sometimes unconscious fear and hatred of both the opposite sex and oneself. Any of the varieties can also be associated with self-hatred.

Homosexuality

Is homosexuality acquired, or is it inborn? Do we attribute sexual orientation to heredity or to environment? What is homosexuality? What is its essence? Where did it come from?

Homosexuality is one of the results of the Fall, just as every other proclivity to sin is. We and our forebears failed. Homosexuality differs little from any other form of sexual sin. It is sexual identity confusion expressing itself in a particular way. Homosexuals may have more extreme forms of sexual identity confusion; but even so, we are dealing with a difference in degree, not in kind.

I have become convinced that there is no such separate condition as homosexuality – just sinners with different forms of sexual weakness and different degrees of identity confusion. People who adopt a homosexual life-style may not like my saying that, wanting us to legitimise their behaviour as a special yet natural condition or state – but I believe it is true. Homosexuals are men and women like the rest of us, and *all* of us sinners are either wrestling with or giving in to our particular sexual vulnerabilities.

Inversion

The word *inversion* means opposite, upside down. To invert something means either to turn that something upside down or to make it do the opposite from what was intended. We were all made sexual for two reasons. The first and I believe most basic reason was that we might know intimacy. 'It is not good for the man [the prototype human being] to be alone,' God muses (Gen 2:18). Intimate relationships are a part of the divine image.

Intimacy, however, glorious as it is and *necessary* as it is, can never be an end in itself. It bursts with onwardness, with creativity, is pregnant with new life. You cannot separate intimacy from life

and creation without destroying it. To separate the
two transforms intimacy into a death's head. If by
our deliberate choice it is not allowed to lead to
life, then in the long run it will produce a degree of
spiritual dying. Creativity, it is true, can partake
of many forms, but in physical human beings it
takes the form of children.

Homosexual encounters, therefore, ultimately
invert both intimacy and sexuality. You cannot
understand sex unless you understand both that
God created it and that he had purposes in doing
so. He planned to multiply his own image in
humankind. He planned also to teach us the
nature of intimacy with himself, that we might
anticipate divine rapture. His still deeper purpose
was to show us the connection between intimacy,
creation and life. Sex is a marvel in itself. It also
serves as a parable, an illustration of the true. It
shows in the natural realm what is true in the
spiritual.

In homosexual encounters, we seek sexual intimacy with no possibility of procreation. Intimacy
of this sort, split from sex and procreation, dies
in isolation. So we kill the thing we crave. All we
then can do is cover the corpse with wax and make
ourselves a mould. If we do not worship the true
God, we have to create – often unconsciously – a
substitute. From the mould we have made, we may
fashion our idol and worship our death mask.

The heart of the moral question lies in whether
God exists and, if he does, what his rights are in
relation to our bodies. If he has rights, what had he
in mind in giving us the gift of sexuality? Whether
a particular tendency is inborn or environmentally
produced is morally irrelevant. Neither in the one
case nor in the other is sinful behaviour excusable.

If homosexual behaviour is sinful behaviour (and the Bible, in spite of attempts to prove otherwise, plainly states that it is), it can be excused neither on environmental nor on genetic grounds. The Bible sees us both as individuals and as a society.

All proclivity to sin is in part inborn. Like David, we, being fallen men and women, are born in sin, 'shapen in iniquity' (Ps 51:5 KJV). If the tendency to sin is genetic, then we must all carry 'sin genes' of various sorts in the cells of our bodies. (How else would we pass our fallenness on to our children?) Yet according to Scripture this hardly excuses our sinful acts. We share in the guilt of our forebears. Even on those occasions when we truly *can* resist sin, we fail consistently to do so.

What matters to God is behaviour. He has compassion on our weakness, whatever form that weakness takes. David compounded adultery with murder, yet he met only compassion *when he acknowledged and repented of his sin*. In Scripture there is no such being as *a homosexual*. There is only homosexual behaviour. It differs in no significant way from any other form of sinful behaviour. Its rapid increase both in society and in the church is one form of God's judgement on us all, judgement for our failure to treat him as truly God.

Because of this, *God gave them over to shameful lusts*. Even their women exchanged natural relations for unnatural ones. In the same way the men also abandoned natural relations with women and were inflamed with lust for one another. Men committed indecent acts with other men, and received in themselves the due penalty for their perversion.

(Rom 1:26–27)

AIDS and those behaviours with which AIDS is associated are not so much a judgement on drug addicts and homosexuals as on society and the church. In any case, AIDS has now spread more widely than addicts and homosexuals. God judges the world. He also judges the church. His judgement is to remove his protection: to *give the world and the church over to* sinful sexual behaviour and its consequences. Why? Because in neither the world nor even the church do we truly acknowledge him as God. In the church we may declare his deity, but we ourselves run the corporation, expecting him to bless us as we do so.

If we wish to be helpful, especially about a homosexual orientation, we must ask whether there is any way of relieving its pain. Is there a release from it? And the answer most certainly is yes. I know that now.

It was this question that most troubled me when I wrote the book *Eros Defiled*.[1] Most of the material in it I still approve of heartily, but there was one answer I sought in vain. I had at that time many homosexual patients, most of whom professed to be Christians. It was their pain that got to me. I had then no answer for it.

I still experience the same pain, the same yearning. The hate and mutual hostility that exist between homosexuals and those who disapprove of homosexual behaviour have increased since I wrote *Eros Defiled*. The social picture is distorted by widespread fear and misunderstanding which, since the discovery of AIDS, grow ever deeper. Those who are pro-gay tend to view the rest of us as homophobic, whether we are in fact so or not. Those who are truly homophobic see homosexuals and their liberal-minded supporters as a diabolical menace to the whole of society, and with rare exceptions lack compassion either for the dilemma of the homosexual orientation or for the fate of men and women who are HIV-positive. Some of these victims are wives and husbands and children, innocent of homosexuality or drug abuse.

The Day I Discovered the Truth

My eyes were opened while I was in California doing research for the book *When the Spirit Comes with Power*. I heard one day of a Los Angeles conference for homosexuals, organised by a local group, Desert Stream. I arrived for the tail end of the conference, where at which about seventy men and women had gathered to listen to the teaching of Leanne Payne. I heard the last part of the last lecture, drank coffee with young people in their twenties and thirties, then attended a time of prayer.

Leanne prayed. If I am not mistaken she prayed audibly but quietly for about forty-five minutes. She seemed to cover a great deal of theological and biblical ground in her prayer. I sensed the presence of the Holy Spirit. Young men and women began to fall on their knees, a few on the floor. Some were weeping.

I cannot remember all that followed, but I had arranged to have supper in a restaurant with the organisers of the conference, all staff members of the Desert Stream ministry. All of them were former members of the gay community, having been free of immoral sexual behaviour for up to a period of seven years. I questioned them closely, one by one, taking careful note of their stories. While none claimed total immunity from temptation, all

testified to a profound difference in their sexual
feelings. Some were by that time married with
children. Others contemplated marriage, having
discovered heterosexual attraction.

The difference was illustrated powerfully a year
or two later when I served as a keynote speaker
at a conference of Exodus International.[2] During
one session I listened to the testimony of a young
lawyer, formerly a member of the gay community.
His conversion had resulted in a conviction that he
must cease from homosexual activity. He was able
to quit the lifestyle 'through gritted teeth.' The
experience had been a grim and painful one – until
he had discovered God's pathway of deliverance.
His face shone with joy and enthusiasm as he
described the relief and freedom that progressively followed. He had not merely reformed his
life. He had been *transformed* by the healing life
of Another.

The Environmental Roots of Inversion

The discovery of a major root of sexual identity confusion is recent. We owe it partly to the
research of Dr Elizabeth Moberly,[3] and partly to
the practical work of Mrs Leanne Payne[4] and
other Christians whose ministry sees men and
women changed in their sexual orientation.

Sexual problems may have many subsidiary
causes, but it now seems likely that one root
cause has unusual importance. Even though the
pattern of events may vary from person to person,
the root cause is probably the same. *Where the
bond linking a child with the parent of the same
sex has suffered damage, sexual identity problems
are likely to occur.*

Psychologist-theologian Moberly re-examined the psychoanalytic literature on homosexuality. As she did so, she discovered a clue she thought might have been missed. Lionel Ovessey, in classic studies dealing with the cause of homosexuality, noted that in all his cases a smothering, overprotective mother was present. He concluded on the basis of this evidence that possessive mothers were the root cause of male homosexuality.[5]

The clue Moberly picked up was in Ovessey's own cases. Not all the boys with overprotective mothers became homosexual. Where the father was active, present and had a good relationship with the boy, that boy did not need to struggle against a homosexual preference. He was 'straight.' In her researches, Dr Moberly began to ask whether the bonding with a member of one's own sex was the key to a homosexual orientation. If it were, could that bonding be repaired?

While not everyone agrees, I suspect that Moberly is right, especially in the case of male homosexuality. More research is needed on the issue of female homosexuality, as anecdotal evidence points to some lesbianism developing as a result of damage some women have endured at the hands of men (such as incest and rape). There may also be many subsidiary causes of sexual identity confusion.

I was sexually molested by a male Christian worker. Even as a young boy, the breasts of women displayed in pictures of primitive people had aroused me sexually. Following my molestation I noticed the same thing about pictures of male nudity. Curiously, in my case it was pictures and statues that aroused me, not the physical presence of naked boys or men. There was little chance of my ever adopting a homosexual lifestyle,

but as I grew older I was aware that I could if I
so chose. I kept fantasies at bay with relatively
little effort, but I sensed within myself that all
was not well.

The nature of my identity confusion lay partly
in the trauma of having to suffer my molester's
shame-arousing, rage-producing advances (I was
unable to tell my parents why I was so reluc-
tant to see him) but an earlier incident was
more basic.

An incident when I was three had destroyed my
trust in my father. He had played a somewhat
innocent joke on me that had the effect of filling
me with fear and rage. (I relate the story fully in
chapter eighteen of *Eros Redeemed* when I discuss
healing of inner wounds.) Suffice it to say for the
moment that the result was that trust was never
fully restored between us, even after the incident
had been forgotten and buried in my subconscious
for decades.

Sometimes the term *bonding* is used to describe
the relationship between two people. Bonding
between children and their parents is important.
Bonding with the parent of the same sex has a
powerful bearing on sexual preferences. Bonding
is that process by which the child *identifies with*
one parent more than another. It is the process by
which the little girl hangs around Mummy when
she is helping others move into an apartment, or
by which the little boy says, 'I wanna work with
computers like Daddy – an' get to use all kinds of
neat stuff.'

I am not, of course, discussing male or female
roles, except insofar as a child's desire for those
roles is a result of attachment to a person. It is
not roles that determine sexual orientation, but

the identification of a girl with a womanly mother and a boy with a manly father.

Ruptured Bonds

Bonds may be impaired in many ways. The damage usually has to do with traumatic experiences of one kind or another. They can occur at any level in the child's development. Damage to a young child will cause more harm than damage to an older child. Again, the more severe the trauma, the worse the damage.

The trauma can be quite mild. Bill had a father who became distant and awkward when Bill reached puberty. Of course, this is a stage at which it is important that the boy receive warm reassurance from his father. 'Hey, your body's developing! Welcome to manhood! You may feel a bit strange from time to time, but you're becoming like the rest of us!' Coming with a hug from a good father who has always maintained a warm relationship with the boy, such a remark can have powerful affirming effects about his developing sexuality, and can open the way to conversations that would never otherwise take place.

Because puberty is a critical time in a boy's development, the effect on Bill of his father's withdrawal was moderately severe. (Bill's grandfather had died at a time when Bill's father was himself just beginning puberty. Thus he had no model for how a father is to affirm a pubescent boy.)

The trauma, mild or severe, can occur through no fault of the parent. Parents can be ill, can have mental breakdowns, can be away for long periods in wartime – and there are other unavoidable reasons. Again, the child may completely

misunderstand the intent of the parent, or the
parent may fail to perceive a need in the child.
A misunderstanding can interrupt effective communication for a lifetime.

Homophobia

I have no doubt that some degree of sexual identity confusion is virtually universal. How could
it be otherwise when none of us receive perfect
parenting, and when all of us as we grow up
misinterpret even the best and kindest actions of
our parents? Some degrees of identity confusion,
especially in more severe cases, lead to the exclu-
sive preferences for persons of the same sex. But
all of us are tarred by it to some degree, and the
forms of sexual temptation to which we are drawn
will vary enormously.

Satan's joke is that our varieties of temptation
determine to some extent the pet hates with which
we regard one another. Yet all of us are victims,
and few of us are pure in our inmost thoughts.
C.S. Lewis put it this way: 'The old Christian rule
is, "Either marriage, with complete faithfulness to
your partner, or else total abstinence." Now this is
so difficult and so contrary to our instincts, that
either Christianity is wrong or our sexual instinct,
as it now is, has gone wrong. One or the other.'[6]
We are damaged in our sexuality.

So what do we say about homophobia? Or about
the hatred on the part of some homosexuals for
'straights'? We must simply say that on both sides
it is naively hypocritical. We are all wounded
by satanic arrows, and our sanctification begins
when we realise our own woundedness and stop
pointing fingers. God's mercy is for all sinners,

even though he loathes all forms of sin. Our proclivity to any and every form of sexual sin is a divine judgement. It is God saying to us, 'If you will not let me be to you all I want to be, you will have to face the consequences. I will not force my love on you. I made you in my image, and I must respect the work of my hands. Only turn to me and I will heal all the damage you have suffered at the hands of the enemy. But you must turn with all your heart.' Those who declare they have no wounds can sometimes be the most wounded of all, the blindest among us.

More to the point, how are we to be healed, sanctified? If you experience homosexual attraction or have adopted a homosexual lifestyle, how can you find the roots of the problem? And having found them, how can they be uprooted? How can you enter into the fullness of your womanhood or manhood? Can you be healed? Of course you can! You are no different from the rest of us.

It involves a biblical understanding of what it means to be masculine and feminine, what memory is (from both a biblical and a scientific perspective) and how the Holy Spirit can work to heal, sanctify and make whole our gender, our memory and our lives.

Chapter 8

Hidden Memories

Who can find a proper grave for the damaged mosaics of the mind, where they may rest in pieces?
I.L. LANGER

The heart is deceitful above all things and beyond cure. Who can understand it? I the LORD search the heart and examine the mind.
JEREMIAH 17:9–10

I have been assuming all along that hidden memories can be the key to helping men and women overcome the proclivity to various forms of sexual sin. Many of these hidden memories concern sexual molestation that happened to people when they were children.

The opening case history in Leanne Payne's book *The Broken Image* is a good example. It concerns a twenty-two-year-old medical student, whom Payne refers to as Lisa. Lisa was homosexual in her orientation, had been suicidal and abused drugs. At the root of her problem was a traumatic event, repressed in her memory for nineteen years. After warning Lisa of the danger of embarking lightly on an attempt to uncover and deal with such a memory, Payne describes what took place.

She was three years or perhaps a little older
in this memory and her own father was . . .
forcing her into acts of fellatio.[1] Her mother
walked into the room and in her hysteria,
rather than handling the situation with the
father and comforting the child, grabbed the
little girl and threw her against the wall. Her
father's words to her mother then boomed out
and resounded once again through her head:
'Aw! she'll never remember!'[2]

Modern Christian literature has many accounts of
this sort, increasing the tension and disagreement
between charismatic Christians and their noncharismatic colleagues over the place of subjective
experiences, and over whether the rediscovery
of a memory can help release us from a sinful
tendency.

What does the Bible teach about memory?
What scientific evidence exists that memories
remain in pure form? Can pseudomemories be
implanted among our true memories? Let me
begin with science (even though I cling to the
old-fashioned notion that theology is the queen
of the sciences and should precede a discussion
of scientific evidence).

The Science of Memory

A good deal of the investigation of memory[3]
reveals how fluid the process of remembering is.
An event we have forgotten, even completely, is
part of the normal working of memory. Therefore,
I must begin by explaining the working of normal
memory.

We remember best whatever we can understand, whatever *makes sense* to us. That is, we

attach our memories to the way we understand the world around us, automatically revising our memories from time to time. Behavioural psychology thinks in terms of learning, of learning to do things – to play the piano, for instance. And behavioural learning affects what we might call narrative memories, or what we might think of as videotapes of the stored memories in our brains.

If there are chemical videotapes in the temporal lobes (or wherever) in our brains, then they are subject to ongoing editing. They are modified by behavioural learning – learning how to do things, learning by experience.

Have you ever noticed the number of arguments that arise when one person describes an incident to others who were there at the time? The arguments can be heated. Psychologists call the memories they are discussing *narrative memories*. Such memories change because behavioural learning affects the way we remember things.

For instance, as I grow from childhood I learn about time partly from repeatedly experiencing time's passage and partly by learning to tell time. Think about small children on a long drive who ask for the twenty-third time, 'When *are* we going to get there, Daddy?' The expression *five hours* does not have the same meaning to a child as it does to an adult or teenager.

New experiences can be understood only in the light of prior memories. Because behavioural learning affects the way I remember, at some point as I recount to a friend an experience from my past I may be a little puzzled. I pause and say, 'No, it *couldn't have been that way*, it must have been' – another way. The manner in which I understand the world around me has changed what I remember, changed it either toward reality or away from it. In this and other ways arguments arise between family members about 'the way it really was.' Therefore, the events subject to recall are not always reliable.

Sometimes we remember things that never happened to us. A parent may have described an incident that took place in our childhood, such as how we reacted when we got a dog as a present. Over many years we may have talked about the event so often that we no longer remember the actual event but only the retelling of the event by someone else. So vividly has the scene been imprinted on our minds that we feel we can remember 'really being there.'

I must not exaggerate the problem or suggest that our memories of past events are entirely erroneous. I suppose most have a lot of truth in them. Yet they are far from being entirely trustworthy.

The History of Traumatic Memories

Disagreements arise over what are called *traumatic memories*, an area in which both the neurosciences and the psychologies are becoming more interested. Recent work among victims of the Holocaust has also awakened interest. Interest is likewise increasing in the work of Pierre Janet.

Janet (not Freud) was the originator of the idea of traumatic memories. He declared that these memories were stored differently from other memories, and recent work in the neurosciences confirms this. Janet was a French neurologist and psychologist who was for a period in charge of the psychological laboratory at the famous hospital of Salpetriere in France. It was he who originated the idea of memories that were sealed off from other kinds of learning, retaining their purer, more accurate form.

While Janet was in Salpetriere, he described a case which exemplified the kind of memory he attempted to explain. Irene, a twenty-three-year-old single woman, attended her mother during her last illness. Irene was deeply attached to her mother, her father being a cruelly abusive alcholic. Whatever money she had earned that could be kept from her father (which was little enough) was spent on food. When her mother died, Irene, her sole attendant during the final illness, had known little sleep for sixty days. Her father, as was the case so very often, was drunk when Irene's mother died. In her exhausted and confused state, Irene could not grasp the fact of the death. She continued to treat her mother as though she were alive, finally pulling the corpse on to the floor in an attempt to get her to straighten out her legs.

Unable to understand what was going on, Irene laughed at the funeral and denied that her mother had died. Her aunt brought her to Salpetriere. On admission she said, 'If you insist on it, I will tell you: "My mother is dead." They tell me that it is so all day long, and I simply agree with them to get them off my back. But if you want my opinion, I don't believe it. And I have excellent reasons for it.' The first excellent reason was that she would grieve deeply if her mother were really dead, and the second, that she loved her mother dearly – and would therefore know.

Now comes the hub of the matter. Though Irene had no memory of the death, she re-enacted it repeatedly. The re-enactment would recur when she saw a bed that seemed to trigger the memory.

As in a trance, she would go through the actions of giving a drink to an imaginary person on the bed, and then a mouth wash, talking to the imaginary person as she did so. For three or four hours a stereotyped behaviour would continue, following an exact sequence during which she would not respond to real people who addressed her. The sequence represented that final three or four hours of her mother's life.

Janet noted that the repetitions of the re-enactment always followed the exact same sequence, lasting the same amount of time. At other times Irene seemed perfectly normal, except for the fact that she appeared to have no memory of her mother's death. Her 'sanity' was touched in only these two ways.

Characteristics of a Traumatic Memory

Pierre Janet characterised the symptoms of a traumatic memory as follows:

1. The memory is maladaptive. It wastes time without restoring the memory to the person who experienced it. Irene would have no recollection of the stereotypical behaviour. Other patients with the syndrome might have nightmares or frightening flashbacks not recognizable as memories.

2. There is no social component. The memory Irene re-enacted was shared with no one. It was not available for sharing in the way narrative memory is.

3. The memory is evoked under particular conditions.

4. If the memory is dealt with as Irene dealt with hers (rather than through flashbacks or nightmares), then once one element is triggered,

the other stereotyped elements automatically follow. This is not true of ordinary memory, where one is free to select a part of the memory from the whole.

Why the trance state? Does one part of her not know what the other part of her is doing? If so, how can the difficulty be resolved (as it eventually was)?

Freud, Janet and Recent Findings

Freud adopted the views expressed and taught at Salpetriere after visiting Janet in 1885, acknowledging the debt in his book *Studies in Hysteria* in 1895. He differed somewhat in that he thought of memory in terms of depth. Dissociated (traumatic) memories were pushed down below the level of consciousness, to emerge in dreams, verbal *faux pas*, word associations, and so on. Janet, on the other hand, had a kind of side-by-side model of memory. He thought of traumatic memories as *split off from the normal learning process*.

Often the terms *repression* and *dissociation* are used synonymously. It is the latter term that reflects the side-by-side model as well as the recent idea of an *alternate stream of consciousness*. A distant memory can be forgotten easily enough, but not split off into an alternate stream of consciousness. Most of the things we have forgotten are of this kind. They have not been 'split off,' but simply forgotten. There have to be extraordinarily traumatic circumstances surrounding the memory for the splitting to take place.

Van der Kolk and van der Hart state:

> Contemporary research has shown that dissociation of a traumatic experience occurs

as the trauma is occurring (Putnam 1989). There is little evidence for an active process of pushing away of the overwhelming experience; the uncoupling seems to have other mechanisms. Many trauma survivors report that they automatically are removed from the scene; they look at it from a distance or disappear altogether, leaving other parts of their personality to suffer and store the overwhelming experience. 'I moved up to the ceiling from where I saw this little girl being molested and I felt sorry for her' is a common description of incest survivors.[4]

Notice – the dissociation occurs *as the trauma is going on*. Tragically, there are some victims of traumatic events who can never resolve the trauma. Many Holocaust victims are among them.

To summarise up to this point, two types of memory seem to exist in human beings. One we call traumatic, the other ordinary. Yet some of the memories which we remember clearly, which we have never forgotten, continue to have power over us, changing our behaviour. These also need to be healed. It is just that we may not have remembered them accurately. The tattered version is all we have. And all we need to be healed from.

As I said above, Payne stressed the need for a thorough grasp of what one is getting into. To deal with traumatic memories is no light matter. It has the possibility of disaster.

Janet used hypnosis (though this is not the way many of us recommend) with Irene to help move the traumatic memory into the realm of ordinary memory. Even so, Kolk and Hart noted,

Whenever [Janet] returned to this subject [of her mother's last hours] Irene started to cry and said, 'Don't remind me of those terrible things. It was a horrible thing that happened in our apartment that night in July. My mother was dead, my father completely drunk, doing only horrible things to me. I had to take care of the deceased and all night long I did a lot of silly things in order to try to revive her.'[5]

Was Irene cured? Was she well? What *is* cure? She had reincorporated the memory into her current experience, but she was still full of pain and distress, unable to stand the pain the memory had now burdened her with. No, she was not healed.

Only the experience of a loving Christ can *heal* such a memory. And this is why I insist on the church's role in such healings. It is also why I declare that healing is a sanctifying process. For Irene was yet to face her resentment against a cruel, selfish and heartless father. She had to know in her experience the love and forgiveness of God her heavenly Father (Mt 6:14–15) and to impact that forgiveness to her own father.

Scripture and the Root of Sin

Remember again Jeremiah's words about our hearts being very deceitful. He reminds us too that a God who is the soul of justice searches its secret depths: 'I the LORD search the heart and examine the mind, to reward a man according to his conduct' (Jer 17:10). God alone knows the depths where secrets lie buried – including split-off experiences we could not face. Therefore, Paul describes himself as doing actions for which he had no explanation, 'I do not understand what I do. For what I want to do I do not do, but what I hate I do' (Rom 7:15).

The existence of the unconscious goes back to the Fall of mankind, when our hearts became deceitful. Who can penetrate their secrets? Only God. Our actions are not the only clue to our conduct. God takes into account the motive – often hidden, even from ourselves. Therefore, the psalmist is forced to cry out in desperation, 'Search me, O God, and know my heart; test me and know my anxious thoughts. See if there is any offensive way in me, and lead me in the way overlasting' (Ps 139:23–24).

David knows perfectly well what his anxious thoughts are. However, he is unaware of the reason for them. He knows what he is anxious *about*, but he does not know *why* he is so anxious. His question is, 'Why am I like this? Could I have offended you? What hidden offence lies buried in my heart to make me like this?' The idea, the principle, has been known for thousands of years. Janet rediscovered or seized on an ancient biblical idea.

Paul wrote, 'My conscience is clear, but that does not make me innocent. It is the Lord who judges me. Therefore judge nothing before the appointed time; wait till the Lord comes. He will bring to light what is hidden in darkness and will expose the motives of men's hearts. At that time each will receive his praise from God' (1 Cor 4:4–5).

In response to the question 'Does the unconscious exist?' John Smelzer says, 'The most significant biblical passage concerning the unconscious, 1 Corinthians 4:1–5, suggests that it does. While Paul is not conscious of anything against himself, he is not acquitted (v. 4). The word "conscious" is the Greek word "sunoida." It means "to know together with" (someone or something).'[6]

You only truly know something when you know it with and in God. We all are thoroughly 'messed up.' The Fall affected our reasoning powers, our emotions, our consciences, so that none of these can be our guide. Therefore Paul, even having a clear conscience, is still not acquitted. God has to examine his heart for things of which he is not conscious. If he is not conscious of something, he must be *unconscious* of that something. As Smelzer expresses it, 'It follows therefore that he must have an unconscious part of his brain which performs without his awareness.'[7]

We forget some things so completely that we no longer have access to them until the Holy Spirit moves in and shows us the 'split-off' portion of our psyches. When that happens it can be devastating. I remember one woman who screamed at what she saw as a split-off memory returned while fellow Christians were praying with her. The memory was of her father holding a knife to her throat during his attempt to rape her during her childhood. There was not only the terrible, burning pain of his attempts to penetrate her immature introitus, but the look on his face, and the knife at her throat. For years her fear of him had puzzled her, often causing her, even when other people were present, to leave a room if her father entered.

Only God has fully tabulated the mysterious dumping ground of fearful memories in some people's brains. Who of us can be sure of their access to the bank of memories stored chemically in our brains? No one. Only God knows them. Only God can heal them. And he longs to do just that.

Chapter 9

Forgiving Family Sin

*The family was ordained of God that children might
be trained up for himself; it was before the church, or
rather the first form of church on earth.*
POPE LEO XIII

*For a son dishonours his father, a daughter rises
up against her mother . . . a man's enemies are the
members of his own household.*
MICAH 7:6

*The family is more sacred than the state, and men
are begotten not for the earth and for time, but for
Heaven and eternity.*
POPE PIUS XI

Family is more important than we think. It has
a greater impact on our lives – for good and
for ill – than we imagine. Both society and the
church lack this understanding because they lack
God's perspective. In this chapter I will consider
how the state (and sometimes the church) can set
children against parents in a destructive fashion
when parents have wronged their children. Then
I will look at how Christians have failed to understand the full extent of the effect of sin from one
generation to the next.

Confrontation

There are times when abuse victims need to confront their abusers, especially when the abuser is an incestuous parent. Of the many means of grace we have focused on, memory healing is unique in the family and it raises unique social issues. We must therefore look at these.

Police and social workers in some areas are anxious to stamp out the great evil of parents molesting their children, and they are often frustrated by the reluctance of children to testify in a court of law against their own parents. This may have value in stamping out a vile social evil, but it may at the same time be destructive to family life, and I am going to argue that there are times when *even a bad family is better than no family*.

Two values clash. One is a healthy sexual environment for the child; the other is the importance of family as a basic building block in society. We do not face a simple issue of right vs. wrong; we live in a fallen society where we must frequently choose between the lesser of two evil choices. Divorce statistics tell us that the integrity of the family is valued little, even by Christians. Divorce, for all the pain of the experience, seems an easier or more attractive option than sorting the marriage out.

The critical question about incest is: At what point do we see a family as having irrevocably destroyed itself? Can incestuous parents be cured? Can they be healed enough to be able to live with their children again? Apparent cures are often followed by a return to the destructive behaviour. Nevertheless, if we abandon the family too readily, we allow society to continue rushing downhill on a self-destructive path.

We can afford to abandon the family only when we absolutely must. Clearly, civil action by society and its appointed representatives is needed to prevent anything of this sort. And yet we must recognise that there are limits to what law can do in reforming society.

There is another danger: The state can be set over and above the family in a destructive fashion. If the law is applied too vigorously, if children are unnecessarily called on to side with the state against their parents (when there is hope for correction or cure), worse damage may be done to the children and to society. Our continued failure to recognise the high value of family will end in destroying society itself, will create chaos – an even greater evil – in an attempt to control the evil we all want to oppose.

God invented family. It arises out of the being and nature of God. Because of this, it is something Satan has always yearned to destroy. Commentators argue about Paul's meaning in Ephesians 3:15, where he talks about the Father 'from whom his whole family in heaven and on earth derives its name.' I believe Francis Foulkes is right when, after careful examination of the Greek text, he says, 'God is not only Father, but he is also the One from whom alone all the fatherhood that there is derives its meaning . . . In effect the apostle is saying, think of any "father-headed group" . . . *in heaven and earth*. Each one is named from Him. From Him it derives its existence and its concept and experience of fatherhood.'[1]

I would add that a family's experience of motherhood also derives its existence and its concept and

experience from God. All parenthood arises in him
– and will therefore be a target for Satan.

We still look forward to a day of restored family
relationships. It is something Christ paid for by
his blood.

Positive Family Confrontation

Let me get back for a moment to the issue of
confronting another family member. A group of
Christians prayed for a woman I will call Janette.
While they were praying, Janette recalled a long-
forgotten conversation with her mother. She was
shocked by the restored memory. The two had
been close, and Janette, then a teenager, remembered she had been sharing with her mother the
anxieties she experienced when she touched her
own genitalia. The mother sought to be reassuring.
But at that point there came a turn in the memory.
In the daughter's memory the mother exposed her
own body to Janette and asked her to touch what
she was exposing.

According to Janette, the counsellors had told
her that the incident explained sexual difficulties
she was experiencing, and instructed her to confront her mother with what may well have taken
place. When Janette, fresh with the recovered
memory, and rejoicing in a healing she professed
to have received, broached the subject, her mother
at once denied that any such thing had taken
place. The conversation, yes, she remembered
clearly. She also remembered Janette's anxiety
about dawning sexual feelings. But she could not
relate to the account of her own exposure, much
less her request that her daughter touch her (the
mother's) private parts.

Janette's mother recounted the matter to me. It was obvious to me that if Janette's memory was a valid memory in its entirety, *the mother herself did not share it*. When I saw her she was not acting a part, but was quite bewildered by her daughter's story, so troubled and bewildered that she had sought me out. Either the exposure was totally blotted from the mother's memory, or else the daughter's memory was a memory containing other ingredients. But if the mother had not exposed herself, how had the 'memory' arisen?

Sometimes there is no way of knowing, but in this case there was a very real possibility. The mother described to me the great difficulty she and her husband had experienced during a number of years. They had once lived in a small house, too small for their growing family. One room of the house was occupied by the woman's mother-in-law, who was senile. The senile grandmother was aware enough to dote on Janette, then only a small child. The friendship was disturbing to the parents, because the old lady perpetually left her door open and occasionally exposed herself, masturbating. They never saw the child with the grandmother on such occasions, but since the child frequently ran into the grandmother's room, and since the grandmother often called to the child and gave her candies, the mother was anxious. The father tended to pooh-pooh the idea that harm could come, which added to a certain tension between husband and wife over the mother-in-law's taking up a room in their little house.

The mother's question was simple. Could her daughter now be confusing two incidents, bringing the two together as one? I had to admit that, yes, that was perfectly possible. It happens all the time.

Let us be clear about two things. First, that God is a revealer of secrets. He reveals accurately and clearly. Second, that visions, words of knowledge, pictures in our minds, even memories come through the filter of our fallen personalities. God is faithful, and will always clarify things when confusion arises. The revelation of a memory under the influence of the Spirit is a communication from God, and as Thomas Keating expresses it, 'One can get into all kinds of trouble. There is no guarantee that any particular communication to an individual is actually coming from God. Even if it is, it is almost certain to be distorted by one's imagination, preconceived ideas or emotional programming, any one of which can modify or subtly change the communication.'[2]

Recovered memories are not Holy Writ. They do not have the infallibility of Scripture. But let us suppose the memory was a real one, not a traumatic one, and that the mother had repressed it. What should she do? Or her daughter? An embarrassing impasse has been created. Mother and daughter stand on either side of a wall that neither of them enjoys and that neither of them wishes to vault. Neither can be certain of the truth.

We must remember who is behind the destruction of family life, and who is the true source of it. The widespread disintegration of Western families, whatever social and legal forces may contribute to it, has a satanic source. If it is to be overcome, it must be by means of an outpouring of the Holy Spirit in revival. And if mother and daughter come together, then it must be by biblical principles. Both must recognise that at present no certainty is possible.

If the mother has repressed a memory, then God can reveal that memory. Nothing will be resolved by an accusatory shouting match.

Or, if the daughter's recovered memory has been polluted by other elements, God can also make that clear. He is in the business of reconciliation. But it may take time. God has his own timetable in our sanctification and healing. We do not know his timetable with either mother or daughter.

It is for the mother to say, 'Darling, I'm glad that this memory helps you. But I really have no memory of parts of it, though I could be wrong. At any rate, I am sorry for any way in which I ever did hurt you, because I love you and don't want to see you unhappy.'

It is for Janette to say, 'Mom, Satan is in the business of breaking up families, and you mean a lot to me. I believe what you say – you really *don't* remember what I think *I* remember. But God still reveals hidden things. Why don't we pray together that God will sort this out for us, and that he will help us resist the temptation to resent each other.'

And both should think twice before sharing the matter any more widely, even in the family. The mother wouldn't want to, unless it were to win support against false accusation. The daughter, on the other hand, could be spreading a false accusation.

I think of three other families that have recently come to me with similar problems. I know that this sort of thing is going to happen more and more, for the underlying problems are common and widespread, and counsellors and churches

are getting in at the deep end in dealing with
it. I admit that the scenario I paint with mother
and daughter would take a lot of grace. But God
is into grace. We are to be on his side where
incest, possible incest and other family abuse
are concerned. We want healed families where
possible, not fragmented ones.

The issue is important, especially where the
church is involved. Church discipline arises out
of a gospel of reconciliation. It is above all things
a reconciliatory procedure, a healing of alienation.
To be such, the heart of the offended person,
the victim, must itself be so drunk with the
glory of Christ's forgiveness that it cannot spare
one cubic millimetre of space for the proud and
self-righteous stance of resentment.

The Family of Love

Not long ago I watched a television programme
featuring a mother's rescue of her children from
their father. The father, who lived with the children in an Asian country, was a member of the
cult known as the Family of Love, once called
the Children of God. The movement, beginning
as an evangelical entity, deteriorated over the
years to something very evil. One of its evils
concerned teaching children 'to share their love.'
By instruction in the family, by the use of frankly
pornographic comic books portraying parent–child
sex acts (in fact giving instruction in erotic behaviour), parents and children of the movement give
themselves to evil.

The quintessence of the evil is that children
are taught that evil is good. They are taught to
see evil acts as holy acts. (What else is new?

This was precisely the evil of the pagan fertility
religions.) But children in the Family of Love are
also instructed never to show the comic books to
anyone outside the movement or to mention what
takes place in the home. During the programme,
as the mother and a TV interviewer questioned
the children, the younger ones freely admitted
what was going on. But when in the interview
the comic book was displayed, an older girl cried
out in obvious distress, 'People are not supposed
to see that! It's not for showing to everyone!' Her
face, her gestures, her distress came through
powerfully. It was as though she were being
the 'good girl,' standing up for what was upright
in the face of an evil mockery of holy things.
What picture, we may well ask, did that girl
have of God?

In *Eros Defiled* I described my own molestation
by a Christian worker who, to my parents' joy,
took me on holiday with him to his own home.
They told me (not realizing what they were saying) to be a good boy, and to do 'whatever Mr
X tells you to do.' What followed was embarrassing, horrifying, shameful. Most humiliating
was the discovery that my pyjama trousers had
disappeared. I felt very strange, naked from the
buttocks down ('Oh, come on! A boy your age
doesn't need pyjama trousers!'), kneeling beside
the bed with Mr X's arm around my shoulder
as we 'prayed' together. It was a bed where we
were also to sleep together. His wife used the
guest room.

Long after he had finished, I lay in bed awake
while he slept. God, I had discovered, dwelt in
darkness. Perhaps there was no God. I could not
find him for a long time after that. At times I

thought I must be very evil. Paul was right.
Children have a deep knowledge about what is
sexually evil. Paul is correct as he writes to the
Corinthians about sex and gender issues. As he
puts it, 'Does not the very nature of things teach
you . . . ?'

Yes, children know. The girl who protested
about the display of the 'sacred' comic books
could be rescued. Beneath the wrong standards
that she had slowly come to accept as right (in
her need to please her father and 'be a good girl')
there lies a deeper knowledge, implanted by her
heavenly Father. But nothing would be gained
by teaching her to deny or hate her father. The
unlearning and relearning that she faced would
take years. She must learn to be loved truly,
learn forgiveness and cleanness, learn to respect
herself, and from the firm basis of knowing love,
forgiveness and cleansing, then learn compassion
for a deceived man.

Parents and children may need to separate at
times, but parent–child bonds are made in heaven,
and we must be cautious about teaching a child to
consider a parent to be an enemy. Certainly in the
case of the Family of Love, the father is a sinner
and may need to be separated from his children.
But that does not end the relationship, and it does
not mean he cannot receive the forgiveness of God
and his family.

The Nature of Mercy

We have no place in our human hearts for the
molester. Contempt, disgust, rejection and even
hatred are the molester's lot. It is what they
deserve, you say. Yes, but so do you. So do I.

Instead, Christ offered us mercy. We all owe a persistent offer of mercy to molested children and even to their molesters. But for molesters it must always be *the mercy of deliverance, and on the evidence of true repentance*. Our debt is to Christ himself, and he asks us to pay it to both sides, to the victims and to their offenders – who were so often victimised themselves in childhood, becoming victims of the malice of fallen angels, victims of darkness and of the forces of darkness, the spiritual hosts of wickedness in heavenly places. Powerless because of the sin in our midst, it is against those spiritual hosts we wrestle so feebly when we preach.

We must walk in forgiveness and teach it. Our model is God the Father. His heart never stops reaching out to the sinner. He is patient, longsuffering, 'plenteous in mercy.' He waits on the rooftop, scanning the horizon for the prodigal's return. Once he is sure who is coming, he rushes to meet him. His prime concern is not the precise degree of repentance. Look at the text of the parable in Luke 15. If you compare what the son planned to say with what he got time to say, you will notice a difference. The father seems to cut off the confession speech before the son finishes speaking, in the overwhelming joy of feeling his son's body, chest to chest, in his arms again (Lk 15:18–22).

The evil of parents who abuse their children in porn parties, the evil of families engaged in witchcraft, the evil of movements like the Family of Love are at least straightforward. Evil is evil. Sooner or later children must resolve their own stance and face their parents. But there are murkier cases, especially when we are dealing with the recovery of forgotten memories involving isolated incidents.

So What Can We Be Sure Of?

You can be sure whether you yourself truly know God's forgiveness. Knowing verses about God's forgiveness does not necessarily mean you really know it in the depths of your being. You can measure your apprehension of God's forgiveness to you *by the ease with which you can forgive others*. Often I hear the words, 'Oh, yes! I know God has forgiven me,' when the actions and attitudes in the person speaking represent a denial of their words. The speakers know forgiveness by intellectual conviction only. They have not experienced its depths with their whole person.

I have taken the trouble to examine this question in detail because I know it will become more and more important as more and more Christians come to terms with memories of past incest. Some already, wrongly instructed by would-be counsellors, refuse to have fellowship with their parents, because the parents will not or simply cannot remember and acknowledge what their son or daughter claims happened in the past. Yet healing is possible even if my parent does not acknowledge the wrong that I say (possibly mistakenly) that he or she did to me. The idea that I cannot forgive (in the sense of experiencing a tender, forgiving attitude) until the person who hurt me has repented is also unbiblical. Only God has that prerogative. It is painful to face an unresolved issue between my parents and myself, but it does not have to be the end of all communication or all expressions of affection.

Healing Hereditary Traits

In discussing sin and forgiveness, we have already moved into the second area in which the importance of the family is not realised, this time by the church.

Many believe that nothing can be done about inherited traits, that one just has to struggle against them with God's help. Already I have pointed out that *both* environment and heredity are sources of your sexual sins and struggles. What is a Christian and biblical understanding of heredity?

I inherited sin. It came to me in my parents' seed. But to understand what this means, we must understand the doctrine of the seed as it is developed in the Old Testament. It is the view adopted by orthodox Jews. According to this view, my seed does not merely refer to the first generation of my children, but also includes the descendants that will follow them hundreds of years from now. It also means that my own seed carries sins from my remote ancestors.

God is the God of families. We think of the earth's inhabitants in terms of nations, of peoples, forgetting that the original human way of looking at them was by generation. Seed has to do with descendants, and descendants with spreading families. God blesses families. The King James version of God's promise should not be forgotten: 'and in thee and in thy seed shall all the families of the earth be blessed' (Gen 28:14).

Your weaknesses to sin have a particular pattern. Stealing may cause you no major temptation, but you may have to struggle against the urge to fool with your little daughter sexually. You've

never done it, but you've come near it at times.
Jim, on the other hand, finds himself slipping his
arm around the waist of every woman he meets,
while Mary's struggle is against bitter jealousy.
People differ in what tempts them most. People of
one ancient city will have a tendency to be more
inclined to drunkenness, whereas another city
may display a greater tendency to homosexuality.
Scots are said to be more prone to resentment and
suspicion, Welshmen to depression and self-pity,
Jews and Chinese to too great a love of money.
There is more than a grain of truth in such
generalizations. The patterns come not only from
wounds in a people's past (sins against them by
others), but from the failures and sins of their
forebears.

God decreed that this would be so. 'The LORD
is slow to anger, abounding in love and forgiving
sin and rebellion. Yet he does not leave the guilty
unpunished; he punishes the children for the sin
of the fathers to the third and fourth generation'
(Num 14:18).

God's ways may seem unjust to us. We have
been indoctrinated with the world's point of view
– and have mistaken it for God's. We have lost
our sense of corporate responsibility, in spite
of the confused web of genetic links that binds
us. God punishes in two ways, first by certain
inevitable consequences that follow a man's or
a woman's sin – the loss of a fortune, the blame
and opprobrium that fall not only on the sinner
but also on that sinner's descendants. Second, God
punishes by a proclivity in future generations to
sin in a particular way. Moabites and Ammonites
were known for sexual sin. From whence came
the grip that Baal worship had on them? After

all, their origin was the incestuous relationship
between Lot and his daughters (Gen 19:35–38).

To understand why this is so, and why biologi-
cal studies now link certain behavioural traits
with genetic anomalies, we need to understand
Scripture's teaching about the human seed. Cov-
enants and promises concern descendants. Unlike
the attitude in modern abortion – a self-centred
concern about the immediate consequence of sown
seed – Scripture looks wider and deeper, having
a concern not only for the child, but for the many
future generations that would have come from the
child. The child in Scripture is seen as the vessel of
the seed, the head of a future line of descendants.
The term *murder* minimises the offence of abortion. To cut off many future generations is even
more serious than killing the one child. We are
all links in a chain. We pass on who and what we
are. Descendants are seen as a God-given right,
and God takes the long-down-the-line view.

Thus Isaiah's lament over the death of the
Servant-Messiah is a lament also over the descendants who would never be born: 'By oppression and judgment he was taken away. *And who
can speak of his descendants? For he was cut off
from the land of the living*; for the transgression
of my people he was stricken' (Is 53:8).

In the same way God weeps over what could
have occurred had Israel obeyed him – if they had
not followed Baal and Molech, had not needed
to be purged by their Babylonian experience of
judgement. *God's promise was not fulfilled to
Abraham in the degree that it might have and
could have been.* Recalling the promise he had
made to Abraham, that his seed would be as the
stars, he says: 'Your descendants *would have been*

like the sand, your children like its numberless grains; their name would never be cut off nor destroyed from before me' (Is 48:19).

Now let us talk about the doctrine of original sin. 'In Adam all die,' Paul tells us (1 Cor 15:22). The doctrine of original sin declares two things: that the consequence of Adam's sin is that I inherit a law or principle of sin inside me, and that it is sin that kills me, makes me mortal. *I* die because *Adam* sinned. My body will rot in a grave because of something Adam did. Thus two things have come down to me through my relationship to Adam: my proclivity to sin and my vulnerability to death. How did those things come down? Clearly through human seed. Sin is in some mysterious fashion passed on from one generation to another by means of infected parents. If this should seem startling to you, it may be that you have never thought through the implications of such biblical doctrines as original sin and the significance of human seed and our essentially bodily nature. So the sins of past generations affect me.

And in just the same way as physical traits from past generations may appear only episodically in a family (great-great-grandfather's nose, great-grandmother's blue eyes), so the proclivity to certain sins will also depend on the particular strains of my heredity that happen to make their appearance in me through what some people call the *blood lines* connecting me with the past.

Often we say, 'He's a real musician. It's in his blood.' It was in *Vanity Fair* that James Crawley made his famous remark about the 'blood, sir, in hosses, dawgs, and men.'[3] Shakespeare gets nearer to the point of inherited sin, when he talks of 'any taint of vice whose strong corruption inhabits our frail blood.'[4]

Confessing the Sins of the Fathers

It would be useless to talk about heredity if no practical gains were to arise from it. Can they? Indeed, yes! To understand how this may be, I need to refer to yet another biblical principle which I have dealt with elsewhere.[5] When godly people intercede for the nation of which they are a part, indeed, whenever we pray about the sins of anyone, *we are to identify ourselves with those sins*, accepting the blame for them as though we ourselves were also to blame.

Study Nehemiah 1, or Daniel 9. You will find that neither Daniel nor Nehemiah, when they mention the sins of their forebears, talk about *their* sins, which *they* sinned. Nehemiah says, 'Let your ear be attentive and your eyes open to hear the prayer your servant is praying before you day and night for your servants, the people of Israel. I confess the sins *we* Israelites, *including myself* and my father's house, have committed against you. We have acted very wickedly towards you. We have not obeyed the commands, decrees and laws you gave your servant Moses' (Neh 1:6–7).

'*We* Israelites, including myself and my father's house, have committed . . .' The sins most discussed in the prophets centre around idolatry (and its sexual implications), violent cruelty and oppression – the social consequences of sexual promiscuity. We have no reason to suppose that Nehemiah had ever practised idolatry, and we can be absolutely sure that Daniel never did. They were not individually guilty, yet because of

their links with their forefathers they shared in
the corporate guilt. And they both acknowledged
this in true repentance, with contrition.

On two recent occasions I have been amazed
when, in reference to specific sins on the part of
parents, grandparents or more remote ancestors,
people have been encouraged to confess those sins,
identifying with their forebears and confessing the
sins as though they themselves also were guilty –
as indeed the Scripture portrays the matter.

One person whom I personally observed said,
'Sure!' and proceeded to confess specific ancestral
sins which he knew of but was not personally
guilty of. No sooner had a few words left his
lips than a sudden awareness broke over him
of the reality of his guilt. Gone was his easy
manner. He began to weep. Before long a look
of wonder replaced the expression of grief, as he
became aware of changes in his being. Behavioural
changes followed in succeeding months, in relation
to the problem that the sins of his forebears
had given rise to. When such identification-based
repentance takes place, the grip of ancestral sin is
broken, and Christians have authority to declare
the chains broken. Chains of sexual sin, too, can
be broken in this way.

After all, this is precisely what Jesus did in
breaking the curse over us. At his baptism he
identified with us *in our sin and guilt*. (The idea
that his baptism was merely 'an example' for us
to follow cheapens the magnificence of his action.)
What else was he doing when he stood in line?
What else, but declare, 'I have come to be one
with you in your sin, to share its guilt'? He was
to be baptised with a baptism of *repentance*. What
need had he for repentance? Did he not hate and

loathe sin? Did not his cousin John, sensing his great virtue, protest the idea of repentance in Jesus? Jesus had nothing to repent *of*, nothing to be released *from*, no chains that needed to be broken. Yet, in order that our chains might be broken, symbolically he repented, identifying with us in our sin, taking our sin on him as a preparation for becoming our sacrifice.[6] It is that very sacrifice by which he wishes to release us from our habitual sexual sin.

Chapter 10

Facing Your Repentant Future

The first step is to realise that one is proud. And a biggish step, too.
C.S. LEWIS

Repentance is the ultimate surrender of the self.
CHARLES COLSON

In Hebrews 11:34 we read of people 'whose weakness was turned to strength.' Only the weak are granted salvation. There is no salvation for the strong. Therefore, if you are strong in sexual matters, read no further. The rest of this book is not for you. Certainly the rest of the book builds on what has been said already about gender and memory. Certainly psychology has a role to play. But no amount of psychological self-help can be a substitute for our weakness before God.

As for the sexually weak, we must cease from our very struggles, which will only cause us to drown. We must desist from the effort even of trying to yield to God. We are to wait and quietly hope for the salvation of the Lord. We cannot take the kingdom by storm. The violent who storm the kingdom are its enemies and will ultimately be crushed. Like weaned children, we wait quietly

for the kingdom's gates to open. Rescuers come
from within. Christ's strength, Paul reminds us,
is made perfect in (our) weakness (2 Cor 12:9). And
weakness waits. It does not cease to hope, even
though hope is almost extinguished, can barely
be felt or recognised. Weakness feebly hopes.
The dawning of hope will be the beginning of a
new day.

Christ, as a human being, is himself the model.
On the cross he met force with weakness. And by
weakness he conquered.

By weakness and defeat, he won the mead
and crown,
Trod all his foes beneath his feet by being
trodden down.[1]

It is the age-old secret of victory when we are
coping with the powers of darkness. We meet our
enemies (pride and force) with weakness, trusting
a mightier arm than our own to save us.

Repentance

Weakness recognises it has no hope in its own
strength. It confesses none is left. All its efforts
have been futile. Augustine began this way when
eventually he came to an end of himself. He found
he was powerless even to face giving up his sin.
Leaving his friend Alypius, he flung himself on
the ground beneath a fig tree, weeping and crying
out, '"And Thou, O Lord, how long? . . . How long
this 'tomorrow and tomorrow'? Why not now? Why
not finish this very hour with my uncleanness?"
. . . So I spoke, weeping in the bitter contrition of

my heart. Suddenly a voice reaches my ears from a nearby house. It is the voice of a boy or a girl (I don't know which) and in a kind of singsong the words are constantly repeated: "Take it, and read it. Take it, and read it."'

He decided that God must have been telling him to take some of Paul's writing that he had been reading moments before. He did so, and opening the book at random his eyes fell on the words, 'Not in rioting and drunkenness, not in chambering and wantonness, not in strife and envying: but put ye on the Lord Jesus Christ, and make not provision for the flesh in concupiscence.' He tells us, 'I had no wish to read further; there was no need to. For immediately as I had reached the end of this sentence it was as though my heart was filled with a light of confidence and all the shadows of my doubt were swept away.'[2]

The time had arrived for God to go to his rescue. The words in the book came to Augustine loaded with divine power. Until that time arrives we must wait, but we shall not wait forever. When words of that sort come we begin to walk along a pathway of repentance. It is a pathway that ends beyond the grave. It is for life. On this pathway we enjoy a growing awareness of our smallness and sinfulness before a very great and altogether holy God. Yet we also grow aware of the results of his full and loving acceptance of us as we are.

I will never stop repenting. At times the repentance will be deep and very, very painful. But the pain will turn into sweet pain, the painful awareness of how greatly I have wounded him, yet of how tenderly, in spite of this, he loves me. At other times it will be a pathway of wonder and worship.

Charles Colson puts it this way:

But the repentance God requires of us is not just contrition over particular sins; it is also a daily attitude, a perspective.

Repentance is the process by which we see ourselves, day by day, as we really are: sinful, needy, dependent people. It is the process by which we see God as he is: awesome, majestic and holy. It is the essential manifestation of regeneration that sets us straight in our relationship to God and so radically alters our perspective that we begin to see the world through God's eyes, not our own. Repentance is the ultimate surrender of the self.[3]

What *is* repentance? I talk about it at great length in another book,[4] feeling that it is grossly misunderstood and mistaught in some Bible schools and even seminaries. I must be cautious and somewhat tentative in offering a definition, but I would say that *biblical repentance begins with a radically changed view of God and of sin (that can be the painful part) and proceeds with a change in direction – a conversion, always winding up in comfort and joy.*

Two questions arise immediately. First, how did that changed viewpoint come about? Who or what was at the bottom of it? Second, many older accounts are filled with distressed and weeping people. Were people long ago more emotional than we now are? How important is the distress?

Perhaps there is yet another question. Repentance and lifelong sanctification are connected. But you say: I thought repentance was something that happened once, when I was converted. Isn't it?

Life and justification are what are given once.
They are given as your faith reaches up to receive
them as gifts, as you trust the word of the Living
One. But you go on turning, repenting, changing
all your life. You will repent about your sexual sins
and stupidities – as well as about every other kind
– to the end of your life. The conversion I speak of
in my definition is not a reference to justification
but to a profound change of habit, behaviour and
attitude towards an aspect of life – in this case
towards sexual sin.

David and Bathsheba

Let me go back to the question of a changed
viewpoint. How did the change in David's viewpoint come about? David's blindness to his own
adultery and murder ended with dramatic sud-
denness when Nathan, impelled by the Spirit
of God, confronted him. Nathan turned David's
burning anger (against an imaginary rich man
who robbed a poor man of his one sheep) against
David himself. Scales were torn from David's own
eyes; his soul was searched with remorseless,
searing light.

"Then David said to Nathan, "I have sinned
against the LORD"" (2 Sam 12:13). For the first
time since he had been daydreaming on the rooftop
he saw his sin with a new and disagreeable clarity,
saw it in the light of God's holiness.

Repentance begins with a revelation by the Holy
Spirit of our sin and of God's love and holiness.
A dramatic intervention is only necessary when
we are resisting that process. Sometimes God
seems to allow our blindness to go on for a while
before he deals with us, allowing us to learn by

painful consequences before he shows us what
we have done. You learn either by consequences
or by illumination. And remember, *the painful
consequences of David's sin remained to the end
of David's life, even though he repented*. But, and
this is what matters, he was restored to fellowship
with God.

Some of us, however, are already overwhelmed
by a sense of guilt, sometimes an unnecessary
sense of it. In that case the revelation is more
of the pardoning love and grace of God. The key
to the process is a tender heart. The heart in
Scripture seems to typify the whole of us, not just
our emotions. But tenderness means *sensitivity*.
A tender portion of your anatomy is a portion
that responds very quickly to pain. Many of us
harden our hearts. That is, we grow hardened,
insensitive to the voice of the Spirit, shielding
ourselves from the pain of seeing. Only God can
soften a hard heart.

Who Does the Repenting?

You say, 'I thought repenting was up to me. You
make it sound as though repentance is something
that happens, something I can't help, that kind of
takes over. Surely it's up to me to face the fact that
I'm twisted sexually and to do something about
it. After all, when Peter preaches his evangelistic
sermon, he talks about repentance as something
his hearers must *do*.' Yes, Peter did say that.
'Repent and be baptised, every one of you, in
the name of Jesus Christ for the forgiveness of
your sins. And you will receive the gift of the Holy
Spirit' (Acts 2:38).

You must certainly face sexual sin, but as for

doing something about it, that is precisely where
the difficulty lies, isn't it? You cannot deliver
yourself from a tendency to mess up sexually
any more than a leopard can change its spots.
Then is repentance something I do? Yes and no.
After all, in that very passage in Acts, Peter is
addressing people *in whom the Holy Spirit has
already produced a terrible conviction of sin*. The
effect of Peter's words was devastating. 'When the
people heard this, they were cut to the heart and
said to Peter and the other apostles, "Brothers,
what shall we do?"' (Acts 2:37).

The process had to begin with a divine action,
a revelation by the Holy Spirit. The same scales
have to be torn from your eyes that were torn from
David's. You have to *see* sexual sin the way God
sees it, and only the Holy Spirit can reveal that to
you. Your grasp of theological principles alone is
of no help. Repentance is a collaboration with God
in what he is trying to do in you. It is God-centred,
not you-centred.

Emotion and Repentance

And that is where emotions enter in. Seeing is
an experience, and when you see things the way
God does, that seeing can be overwhelming. I am
against emotionalism, but I must continually bear
in mind that God created me an emotional being.
Of course, too much emotion is bad. But then,
too little can be the sign of approaching insanity. And most well-educated people of northern
origins suffer from too little. We are cool cus-
tomers whose upper lips are stiff – along with
our necks.

Charles Finney (many aspects of whose theology

leave me disturbed) hits a bull's-eye in his description of the repentant person: 'In relation to God, he feels towards sin as it really is, and here is the source of those gushings of sorrow . . . when he views it in relation to God, then he weeps; the fountains of his sorrow gush forth, and he wants to get right down on his face and pour out a flood of tears over his sins.'[5]

I know that the end result of repentance is a change of mind and changed patterns of behaviour. But those changes come about in relation to our being awakened to reality. The reality can produce something Paul calls 'godly sorrow.' Mere weeping is not to be equated with repentance. Paul was very clear about that. 'Yet now I am happy, not because you were made sorry, but because your sorrow led you to repentance' (2 Cor 7:9).

Repentant weeping is *godly* weeping. There are two kinds of weeping in Pauline thinking, two kinds of sorrow – godly sorrow and worldly sorrow. Sorrow that leads to repentance is godly sorrow. True emotion is no enemy of faith, only emotion of a wrong kind, or for the wrong reason. Grief, too, comes in two varieties: godly grief and worldly grief. As Paul explains, 'For you became sorrowful as God intended and so were not harmed in any way by us. Godly sorrow brings repentance that leads to salvation and leaves no regret, but worldly sorrow brings death' (2 Cor 7:9–10).

Repentance is a note too often missing from the melody of the gospel. *Saving faith can arise only in the context of true repentance.* The depth of emotion that so often accompanies repentance can be a measure of both the reality of understanding and the behavioural changes that follow it. Repentance alone can be enough to secure deliverance from some sexual bondages and addictions.

I am so grateful that Charles Colson (of Watergate fame) has left us an account of the night of August 12, 1973. It has nothing to do with sex, for sex is not what God is dealing with at this point in his life. Rather, Colson is sitting in his car in the dark. He has left politics for law, little dreaming what the future holds. He has just spent time with Tom Phillips, president of Raytheon, the largest employer in New England and one of Colson's clients. Phillips has recounted to Colson the story of a revolution in his life and has read him a chapter from C.S. Lewis's book *Mere Christianity*. Colson records his feelings as he leaves the house.

Outside in the darkness, the iron grip I'd kept on my emotions began to relax. Tears welled up in my eyes as I groped in the darkness for the right key to start my car. Angrily I brushed them away and started the engine. 'What kind of weakness is this?' I said to nobody.

The tears spilled over and suddenly I knew I had to go back into the house and pray with Tom. I turned off the motor, got out of the car. As I did, the kitchen light went out, then the light in the dining room. Through the hall window I saw Tom stand aside as Gert started up the stairs ahead of him. Now the hall was in darkness. It was too late. I stood for a moment staring at the darkened house, only one light burning now in an upstairs bedroom. Why hadn't I prayed when he gave me a chance? I wanted to so badly. Now I was alone, really alone.

As I drove out of Tom's driveway, the tears were flowing uncontrollably. There were no street lights, no moonlight. The car headlights were flooding illumination before my eyes, but I was crying so hard it was like trying to swim underwater. I pulled to the side of the road not more than a hundred yards from the entrance to Tom's driveway, the tyres sinking into soft mounds of pine needles.

I remember hoping that Tom and Gert wouldn't hear my sobbing, the only sound other than the chirping of crickets penetrating the still of the night. With my face cupped in my hands, head leaning forward against the wheel, I forgot about machismo, about pretences, about fears of being weak. And as I did, I began to experience a wonderful feeling of being released. Then came the strange sensation that water was not only running down my cheeks, but surging through my whole body as well, cleansing and cooling as it went. They weren't tears of sadness or remorse, nor of joy – but somehow tears of relief.

And then I prayed my first real prayer. 'God, I don't know how to find You, but I'm going to try! I'm not much the way I am now, but somehow I want to give myself to You.' I didn't know how to say more, so I repeated over and over the words: *Take me*.

I had not 'accepted' Christ – I still didn't know who He was. My mind told me it was important to find that out first, to be sure that I knew what I was doing, that I meant it and would stay with it. Only, that night, something inside me was urging me to surrender – to what or whom I did not know.

I stayed there in the car, wet-eyed, praying, thinking, for perhaps half an hour, perhaps longer, alone in the quiet of the dark night. Yet for the first time in my life I was not alone at all.[6]

The Supremacy of Grace

What happened to Chuck Colson happened because of grace. The grace that God gave him on that occasion was what theologians call *prevenient* grace, grace that comes to us *before* we find Christ, and without which we will never find him at all. You will notice that in the account above he makes that absolutely clear: 'I had not "accepted" Christ – I still didn't know who He was.' We need the grace of God all our lives. Every time the Spirit shows us things, it is an act of grace.

Grace puts us in touch with reality. Most of us are not in touch with reality at all. We think we are but we're mistaken. To be exposed to the awesome realities of eternity is devastating. Poor old Ezekiel, after seeing the glory of the Lord, tells us, 'I sat . . . for seven days – overwhelmed' (Ezek 3:15). We think we know about lost souls. We don't. If we did we would be like Ezekiel – overwhelmed. We think we know the horror of our own sexual sin. But we're wrong. If we once caught a glimpse of it, we'd be just as overwhelmed as Ezekiel.

Only occasionally have I seen glimpses of what lies beyond. It is more than I personally can handle. For three seconds (I would guess) I once saw the coming judgements of God on Canada.

The vision was sudden. I struggled out of the armchair I was sitting in and yelled, 'No, God, No! You mustn't do that! Stop! STOP!' I found myself with my hand raised and was shocked. Quickly, I sat down, frightened at what I had seen and at my own instinctive reaction. People around me were startled – we were in the middle of a prayer meeting, and I was embarrassed. But I shall never forget what I saw.

No. We do *not* live in reality; we are mercifully shielded from it. God has to let us have small glimpses of our personal reality. He shows us what our sin looks like in small doses. Even his love overwhelms us when he lets us catch a little glimpse of it. Our eyes are opened to reality, by grace, a little at a time.

The Approach to Repentance

You say, 'I'm still not satisfied. You tell me the process has to begin with the illumination of the Holy Spirit. How do I get that? How do I make the process start?'

At last we have arrived at the real starting point. *You cannot make it start*. God has to start the process – and he has probably already started. If you doubt that, then your part is simply to ask him to grant you repentance, to soften your hard heart, to open your eyes. He will not necessarily do so the moment you ask, but trust him. If you really mean business, there is no question that he will start at once – assuming that he has not already started.

But do not delay. In the mind of the writer to the Hebrews, sexual immorality is coupled with giving up one's birthright. Notice what Hebrews

says: 'See that no-one is sexually immoral, or is
godless like Esau . . . Afterwards, as you know,
when he wanted to inherit this blessing, he was
rejected. He could bring about no change of mind
[RSV, 'he found no chance to repent'], though he
sought the blessing with tears' (Heb 12:16–17).

Two things are apparent. First, you cannot
bring about a change of mind in yourself about
sin, sexual or otherwise. You cannot see as God
sees unless he opens your eyes. Second, weeping
is not at the heart of repentance. You can weep all
you want and get nowhere. If God opens your eyes
you may weep, or be shocked, or experience merely
a gentle moving of the Spirit of God and be filled
with wonder and awe. And the experience will be
repeated again and again as long as you live and
are tender towards him.

Ask God to give you what you need. Ask him to
open your eyes. Sooner or later the process will
begin. But do not delay to ask. Take the stance
of a penitent. Tell him, 'Lord, I recognise that my
sexual carryings-on displease you. I know they are
wrong and that I've grieved you. Help me to see
them as you see them.'

He may take some time in doing so, but in the
end you will not be disappointed.

Chapter 11

Prayer: A Means of Grace

*In this humanistic age we suppose man is the
initiator and God the responder. But the living Christ
within us is the initiator and we are the responders.
God the lover, the accuser, the revealer of light and
darkness presses within us.*
WILLIAM KELLY

*Do not be deceived: Neither the sexually immoral
nor idolaters nor adulterers nor male prostitutes
nor homosexual offenders . . . will inherit the
kingdom of God. And this is what some of you
were.
But you were washed, you were sanctified.*
1 CORINTHIANS 6:9–11

Sexual sin can eventually become to the struggler what the ocean is to a drowning man. You
struggle as if your life depended on it, alternately
struggling and despairing.

I learned about lifesaving as a schoolboy, even
winning the silver medallion (the highest award) in
a lifesaving contest. I remember that in training we
had to learn how to deal with the drowner's struggles, how to break various kinds of holds, the holds
with which a desperate struggler would seize us.

Christ seems to have another technique. He waits

till the right moment before rescuing. He alone
knows when that moment comes. For a drowning
person, this can be terrifying. If you cannot do
anything else, you can and must struggle, must
fight to keep your head above the surface. You
battle despairingly to resist terrible forces pulling
you down. To give up is unthinkable. In fact you are
not thinking at all. A deeper instinct has taken over
– one which you are powerless to resist.

Augustine (as mentioned in the previous chapter) had got to that stage. There had been a time
when he simply gave way to his sins of 'wantonness and chambering,' but as he faced the claims of
Christ he saw two things. First, that Christ's way
was the right way, the only way Augustine could
receive him; second, that he had not the strength
to deal with the terrible lust that gripped him.
It was too much a part of him. To quit would be
the equivalent of tearing out his own intestines,
his lungs, his heart. Sexual sin and sins of other
sorts were part of himself. Overwhelmed, he lay
under the fig tree, weeping bitterly. To Augustine
it seemed like an impasse.

There is a form of prayer that expresses this
kind of despair.

It waits before God in silence. The author of the
book of Lamentations speaks of it. 'It is good to
wait quietly for the salvation of the LORD . . . Let
him sit alone in silence, for the LORD has laid it
on him . . . For men are not cast off by the LORD
forever' (Lam 3:26,28,31).

So we wait. Despairingly. *Before God*. And this
waiting is not only a beginning. It is to become a
way of life, a life that recognises its own weakness,
its own powerlessness, its utter hopelessness.
Even prayer – any prayer – must be impregnated

with this understanding. Prayer is nothing if not the admission of my helplessness before God. Yet when I speak of prayer, I am thinking about a particular aspect of prayer, the kind of prayer in which we learn to hear God speak.

Two Kinds of Prayer

It is that form of prayer, above all others, that God is able to use to deal with our sexual struggles — if only we will have the patience to learn it. Do you trust him? Do you believe that he knows the miserable grip that sex has on your life and that he already has a plan specifically for you? He knows about all of your sin, all of your struggles, and whether or not he immediately does exactly what you want him to, he will get around to it in his own good time.

All prayer is an expression of helplessness. Yet when we talk about prayer we distinguish not two, but many, varieties, talking about petitions, supplications, intercession, confession, worship and so on. All must be characterised by the awareness of our weakness. Yet all of them can be divided into two basic varieties which Andrew Murray calls the *family* and *business* varieties.

> If I am in a strange land, in the interests of the business which my father owns, I would certainly write two different sorts of letters. There will be family letters giving expression to all the intercourse to which affection prompts; and there will be business letters, containing orders for what I need. And there may be letters in which both are found. The answers will correspond to the letters.[1]

And of the two varieties of prayer, it is the family kind that matters the most. For if the family is broken, what good does it do them that the business is successful? Why should it matter if it fails? Where do our values lie? Certainly, in spiritual matters, a broken church is of much less value to a broken world than a church united at its very heart. That is why, in his high-priestly prayer, Jesus besought the Father for unity, 'so that the world may believe that you have sent me' (Jn 17:21). Only the Holy Spirit gives us such a church. And this is how the world comes to faith.

Family prayers are those that have to do with tenderness and love, with the intimate relationship with Christ himself which I rediscover every time God rescues me. The kind of prayers that most characterise this attitude are confession, worship, praise, adoration, the general ability to be silent in God's presence and to hear his word as he speaks to our hearts. Business prayers include supplication and intercession. There are thus two sorts of prayer, each dependent on the other. *For you have to be effective in both if you are to have real 'success' in either.*

People who most get answers to prayer are people who hear from God, for in their brokenness they long to hear. The fact that they actually do hear from God becomes evident by the answers they receive. It is the proof that they hear correctly, for prayer is collaboration with God, his strength perfected in our weakness. You may, for instance, claim to hear from God when you are merely listening to your own deceitful heart. If so, you are unlikely to receive answers to your pleading, since answered prayer is prayer that is according to God's will. You have to know his will, both in Scripture and as the Spirit speaks to your heart, if you are to ask things that

God will answer. He acts and we respond. *He has the masculine role, we the feminine.*

This sort of prayer can be learned. Impossibly difficult? No, for the Holy Spirit is a teacher who is anxious to teach you. Ask him to do so. He longs to lead you gently into the ways of effective communion with God, a communion which will revolutionize your Christian experience.

I do not say there will be no times of difficulty, but I do insist that God himself longs to teach you. And sooner or later he will start to get at your sexuality. Once you are ready he will not waste a moment.

God's Voice

I have never heard God through my physical ears. Some people have. Most people have an inner impression, which is my own experience. Sometimes I 'hear' actual words in this way, but just as commonly it is a nonverbalised impression. However, with increasing experience I am able to put words to those impressions with growing accuracy. The expressions, 'I want you to . . .' and 'Would you like to . . . ?' are quite different, and I have experienced both. The distinction is important. Yet with practise it can be discerned. The great evangelist George Whitefield had such impressions, but was persuaded by Jonathan Edwards not to heed them. In my view, this was unfortunate.

But what I have learned in prayer under the tutelage of the Holy Spirit is burned far more deeply into my soul.

John Bunyan emphasises the point. His own pastor, a man named Gifford, had taught him, 'For, when temptation comes strongly upon you, if you have not received these things with evidence from heaven, you will soon find that you do not have that help and strength to resist that you thought you did.' Bunyan states:

> This was just what my soul needed. I had found out by sad experience the truth of these words. So I prayed to God that in nothing related to his glory and my own eternal happiness would I be without the confirmation from heaven that I needed. I clearly saw the difference between human notions and revelation from God.[2]

The principle is true also of sexual temptation. You cannot resist sexual temptation in an area that the Holy Spirit has not revealed to you personally from Scripture.

I have adopted Bunyan's rule for myself. Though I have read through the Bible more times than I can count and have a good notion of its contents, it is only those portions through which God has spoken to me powerfully that assist me when I grapple with the powers of hell. These have become weapons I can count on.

Positions in Prayer

You may have been taught to kneel rather than sit to pray. I usually begin by sitting. I may later be found kneeling or standing, lying on my face or walking. I may be silent, or anything but silent, may shout or sing. My arms may be raised or at my side. But mostly I sit quietly.

You should note two things about position. First, your mood changes subtly with the position of your body. I do not adopt any of these positions consciously. Only as I reflect afterward do I realise my physical behaviours during prayer. To stand with head up and shoulders back makes for a different mood than lying on your face. Second, and perhaps more important, you express differing emotions by your body posture. To lie on your face says, 'I am overwhelmed. How dare I raise my eyes to you?' A time of prayer is a time when you should feel freedom to move.

Transformation

It is still important to grasp that God *wants* to teach you. My own constant battle is to remember that God cares, that he wants to teach *me*, that I do not need to hang back in guilt and shame. Over many years a slow transformation is taking place in me in relation to my sexuality. Looking back, I can now see that it has been God who has been pursuing me, but at the time I thought in my despair that *I* was pursuing *him*. There were times when I would grow discouraged and would neglect times with him. Then I would come across some book or other that would awaken the longing that had begun to grow in me and would start me off again.

Everything began with a commitment on my part – first a commitment to spend time in his presence, then, later, a commitment to learn to listen. Yet from my earliest years I had heard. *I was not consistently faithful to my own commitment*, but God was faithful.

Eventually there came a point when I could no longer tolerate his absence, when the longing for his presence, though it still waxed and waned, would not go away at all. At times it grew almost unbearable and I would cry out. Yet I cannot point to any time or incident when the intolerance began.

At this point in my life I have the faith and the patience to wait on him, knowing that, while I may not be experiencing marvellous raptures, I am always in his presence. Then I hang on, sometimes in stillness, sometimes worshipping quietly, at other times interceding. Slowly, over many years, prayer (the prayer that brings me healing) has been transformed. And when God chooses to draw near (an experience I have no control over), there is no way I can convey the glory. Yet I feel like the merest beginner. I not only feel it. I know it. For all of us are beginners and nothing more than beginners.

How the Process Began

I suspect the beginning of the process of transformation, which took place while I was still a medical student, was my discovery that there were portions of the Bible that made me angry. Usually some action of God in the Old Testament would do this. Before that, a lot of my prayer would amount to religious posturing. I would be busy trying to adopt the correct stance (appropriately respectful and reverent). Finally I allowed myself to get mad: 'Lord, why did you do that? I – forgive me, but *I don't like that in you*! It scares me. Why are you like that?'

I would experience the fearful feeling that I didn't like the God I was seeking. But, though I was terrified, I had no other God. There *was* no other. The only true God was the one I was stuck with! Again and again I found myself saying (in fear and bewilderment) 'Lord, I'm mad at you! I don't want to be, but I am! I know I've no right to be, but I can't help it.'

On many of these occasions he would draw near. He would never explain himself. His very presence was the answer, stilling my heart, humbling me, changing me. If you question the appropriateness of my talking to a holy God like this, I can only say two things. First, to have acted otherwise would have been to add insult to injury. It would have been to pretend, to add a lie to my true, rebellious feelings, even to fool *myself* about my feelings. But I would not have fooled him. In any case, my anger could not damage him.

But there is something else. Read the psalms of David and notice his reactions to God. Notice his reaction at the threshing floor of Nacon (2 Sam 6:6–11). Read Job's terribly bewildered reaction in his grief and pain, in Job 16:7–18. And read Jeremiah 20:7 – 'O LORD, you deceived me, and I was deceived; you overpowered me and prevailed.' This is how Scripture's giants of the faith behaved.

We say, 'Come on! How can we compare ourselves with the greats of Scripture?' *Precisely at the point of their simple honesty before God*! As I grew more honest, treating him like a real person rather than a heavenly blob before whom I was 'reverent,' he became to me that real person.

When God Begins to Speak

In my personal experience, ninety-five per cent of what God says has to do with his efforts to change me. Only five per cent is for other people, and that five per cent is a very frightening five per cent.

How would you react, for instance, if you were addressing a group of evangelical Christian leaders and God were to say, 'See that man there? He's in an active gay relationship. The man on the second row on your left is also. And the two men sitting with an empty seat between them in the back row have similar problems'? That actually happened to me.

Yes, but you are more advanced at this sort of thing, you may say. *It is not a matter of being advanced, but of being willing to obey.*

When God spoke to me about the homosexuals in the conference, I hated the experience. I was not ready to receive that sort of communication. In any case I am chicken when it comes to embarrassing situations. I didn't want to know whether my prompting came from God or not – not in the middle of an address about something entirely different! I concluded that it was 'just my own imagination.'

I did nothing about it then, but the next morning I had to. God would not let me wriggle out of it. The result was that seven homosexual relationships came to light.[3] They included those four men, three of them members of a senior committee in a well-known Christian organization. Within another twenty-four hours I was receiving telephone calls from desperate women who were saying, 'Look, I've got a sexual problem and I just have to see you.' Yes, God opens up ministry through his words to us at times. But remember, I said that ninety-five per cent of the words are *for me*, to clean me up sexually.

Is it not possible to be mistaken about God's voice? To think we hear it when we are deceived? Indeed it is. John of the Cross warns us against

the dangers. That is why you must *learn* to hear.
How can you know when you hear correctly?

Already I have pointed out one way – by the fact
that your prayers, prayers that arose from hearing
God's voice, are answered. Or by the fact that
subsequent events prove you are right. Another
golden rule is that since God is self-consistent,
what he says in our hearts will never violate
Scripture. You just have to be willing to look
like a fool. Anyone can make a mistake. It is
more important to learn to hear God than not to
look like an idiot.

In any case, how could I know 'what the Bible
said' in the case of the men who were in active
homosexual relationships? How could I know that
they really were doing what the Spirit told me?
The only way I could know was by sticking my
neck out, running the risk of looking both very
foolish and very unfeeling. I had to forget about
my dignity. But I had not been deceived. The
men God spoke to me about were among the ones
who came to light. It was rather like diving from
the ten-metre board when the pool looks empty
and discovering that it is full only when you hit
the water.

Solitude

To hear what God is saying calls for *solitude*
and *silence*. If you are broken enough, desperate enough, you will do anything. Abba Anthony
(c. A.D. 251–356) was one of the desert fathers who
fled from civilization because he saw it as a corrupt
and sinking ship where true Christianity could not
flourish. But in the desert he discovered that he
had not escaped anything. He had brought the

world and its corruptions with him into the desert.
He had been moulded by them and they were part
and parcel of his character.

I remember seeing pictures of the temptations
of Saint Anthony in paintings by Hieronymus
Bosch (c.1450–1519). If I understood the paintings
aright, Anthony's temptations – at least in the
vivid and lurid mind of the painter – included
sexual ones. There was a hideous, ghastly beauty
about the sexual aspects of the temptations.

Anthony spent twenty years in solitude, wrestling with his own character and with the terrible
onslaught of temptations he suffered, determined
that Christ would have his way in him. In the
words of Henri Nouwen, he returned to civilization after those twenty years 'an authentic,
"healthy" man, whole in body, mind and soul,' to
whom people flocked for counsel and instruction.[4]
Commenting on this experience, Nouwen writes,
'We must be made aware of the call to let our false,
compulsive self be transformed into the new self of
Jesus Christ . . . solitude is the furnace in which
this transformation takes place . . . it is from this
transformed . . . self that real ministry flows.'[5]

Was twenty years necessary? Does this mean we
must go to the desert for twenty years if we are to
be transformed? What biblical examples are there
of solitude of such a magnitude?

Well, there are some, though the time the individuals spent was shorter. Jesus spent forty days
in fasting and prayer in the desert. Paul the
apostle spent three years in the Arabian desert
(Gal 1:17–18) while John the Baptist spent an
unspecified number of years there.

Revelation (hearing God) and transformation
of character go hand in hand. But the heart of

solitude lies within ourselves. It is more important
to spend time in silence daily before the living God.
Begin with just five minutes. Going into the desert
may have value, but it seems to be the call of
exceptional people. In previous chapters I have
testified to experiences I have had personally
which led to character transformation. Each was a
learning with my whole self (not with the intellect
alone) of lessons that the Holy Spirit taught me in
the early mornings.

Will it take you that long? Perhaps longer. Take
sexuality alone: it may be that there is only one
thing that you think is bugging you. You do not
know a quarter of what is wrong with you sexually.
Once God starts to work on you, you may be very
surprised. I thought there was only one very minor
thing wrong with me sexually when I wrote *Eros
Defiled*. Was I ever surprised once God started on
me! He wanted to make me like Christ.

He wants to do a thorough job on us, to 'do
it right.' Nothing less will content him. He is a
perfectionist in the very best sense of the term, one
whose standards are perfect, as he alone can be.

Silence and Stillness

Running across the surface of your mind every day
is an endless stream of thoughts, of words, a jum-
ble of imaginary conversations, arguments, situations, ideas, hopes, fears and worries – including
sexual stuff. Thomas Keating[6] calls the stream
the *false self*. The true self, the core of your
being, is *you in Christ*. It is not the mere gar-
bage that emerges on the surface of your mind.
Prayer involves learning to detach oneself from
the unending stream of thoughts on the surface

(which is by no means easy) and finding one's way down to the meeting place with God, to the real self-in-Christ.

For you died, and your life is now hidden with Christ in God (Col 3:3)

> We were therefore buried with him through baptism into death in order that, just as Christ was raised from the dead through the glory of the Father, we too may live a new life.
>
> (Rom 6:4)

For it is there, in that sanctum where time and eternity meet, that place in your inner being where Christ and you have been made one, that the transforming instructions are given. That is where you must meet him. But you must accept the fact that God's order in delivering you will not necessarily be the order you would choose. Those sexual tendencies that most humiliate you may not be the ones God deals with first. He will get to them when the time is appropriate. It may well be that you have one or two preliminary exercises to learn first. But sooner or later he will get around to what concerns you the most.

For instance, it was passivity that caused me to struggle in silence and growing hatred against the Christian worker who molested me. I failed to shout to attract his wife's attention partly from embarrassment, but also because I was passive. I preferred to conduct my struggle with my molester in silent hate. My passivity was inherited from my father, an expert amateur boxer who was aggressive in the ring but passive in the home. I had overreacted all my life against the passivity in me by being too aggressive. The underlying passivity undermined my manhood, made me both manipulative and unnecessarily aggressive rather than loving – even in a sexual relationship.

One day in the silence, as I waited on him, God spoke. 'Why do you not accept your father's passivity? After all, it is in the genetic code of your body.'

I was alarmed, and a little angry. I knew I have never accepted it. I did not have the least desire to. I was too busy fighting a tendency I hated and wished to overcome. I asked, 'Of what use is my father's passivity to me?'

The words that came back hit me hard. 'I cannot deal with something you deny you have. It must first be brought to me.'

I thought for a while, knowing that what he said was true. Finally, feeling rather depressed, I said, 'Okay. You're right. I accept it.'

Immediately, as it were, 'through' the back of my head, I could 'see' standing behind me a long line of shadows. They were the shades of the men from whom I had descended. A sorry lot. But *they were the route God chose to bring me into this world*. I knew then that you cannot be a man apart from a context, the context of your own male ancestors. Christ can redeem only what is *there* in us and we are willing to bring to him. He cannot (or does not choose to) change our ancestors. But he can and does change us.

But where can we find the time to let him do so? Obviously it takes time. *We already have that time*.

We are too enslaved to the world's programme of rush and hurry to realise it.

Silence, Stillness and Life's Hectic Pace

We rush because we are enslaved. Anthony Bloom talks about 'moments when you have absolutely nothing to do,' and finds in such moments one test of our enslavement *to* and *in* time. Let me give you an example.

Frequently I arrive in an airport in a late-arriving plane. I have to hurry to the gate of my connecting airline, and I dodge between people coming from the opposite direction, hoping I will not arrive too late at the gate. I get there – and behold, the ongoing plane is delayed for half an hour with some mechanical difficulty. From long experience I know that the half-hour delay could be extended considerably before the problem is rectified. Suddenly I have been switched from rush and hurry to having an unknown amount of time on my hands.

Purely from habit, I open my briefcase. Perhaps I will find a solution to my restlessness inside it. I could read a book – preferably one easy to read – or glance through a magazine. Or I could get some files out, because I have work I could do.

What is happening to me at this point? I have time on my hands and I prefer to fill it with work (I am a workaholic) or with some form of distraction (I am lazy). But I know what God calls me to do because I know something about the experience of his presence. I could seek God's face as I sink into the rest of the joy of the eternal silences. I could do so *not as a religious duty*, but as an exercise in learning not to be enslaved to time.

Yet a strange reluctance seizes me. Do so here? My thoughts are all over the place. Won't it be impossible? I shrink from the effort. For some curious reason, I shrink from the very thing I most need: peace and quiet, the sense of the Holy Presence. I'm not in the mood. I am suffering the penalties of my enslavement to time and its corresponding fear of eternity's calm.

Sighing, I start. I remember that the omnipresent God is present even here. I also remember that by his Spirit he dwells in my own body. His whole Person is in me and yet he is, as Creator and Sustainer, all around me. Soon, hope and a smidgen of peace steal into my heart and I murmur, 'Oh, thank you, Lord!' My mind fluctuates between my circumstances, fragments of conversation with the clerk . . . and God's presence. From habit, now, I keep letting other thoughts go their way and turning them back to God. A few minutes later and without thinking, I stretch hugely, then sigh contentedly and relax. I murmur with real feeling, 'I bless you, Lord!'

Some time later there is another announcement. I do not bother to consult my watch. The loudspeaker asks people who have small children or who need assistance to present themselves. Then, in no time, there is an announcement affecting me. I find myself stretching again before getting to my feet. I am smiling – smiling at the people to whom I give place as they hurry to be first in line. Curiously, I almost love them, aware in my heart that I am loved myself. I am one step nearer to being freed from the bondage of time and the fear of eternity, for, however dimly, I have been drinking a little of its peace in God's presence.

The Inner Sanctum

The sanctum within is a place of silence and stillness, so silence and stillness are what we must seek. It is a quiet, restful place. Stillness and silence make solitude a reality. Solitude, stillness and silence facilitate hearing God's voice. There is a hymn we often sing as a mood song (a bad use of a hymn) without any real anticipation of its request being answered. Or if our hopes do lie in that direction, we confine those hopes to the time of the meeting or church service at which we sing.

> Speak, Lord, in the stillness,
> While I wait on Thee;
> Hushed my heart to listen
> In expectancy.
>
> Speak, O blessed Master,
> In this quiet hour,
> Let me see Thy face, Lord,
> Feel Thy touch of pow'r.[7]

The hymn writer is plainly describing something she herself knew by experience. It is something you can know, too, something God's loving heart longs to share with you. It is for ordinary Christians, not just for advanced mystics. It is the prerogative of every child of God. There are ways of learning how to find it, and in the appendices I have included a list of helpful books. But do not wait until you have read a book. Seek God in the stillness today. Already he seeks for you.

Yet why does the surface of our minds so run with words? What is it about our culture, apart from rush, that makes for such intense difficulty when we seek silence? Henri Nouwen says we are 'inundated with words.' He tells us that once when he was driving on a Los Angeles freeway, he got the impression he was driving through a large dictionary. 'Wherever I looked there were words trying to take my eyes from the road. They said, "Use me, take me, buy me, drink me, smell me, touch me, kiss me, sleep with me." In such a world, who can maintain respect for words?'[8]

Sexual temptations especially come through words and the images they conjure up in our minds. *They come even when we seek the silence of God's presence.* Today a Christian woman was telling me, 'The time is so short. I feel I must stop fooling around. But my mind is so full of impure thoughts.'

I said, 'Tell Jesus about them. He knows, anyway! Tell him, "This is the way I am." Don't feel so bad about it. Don't resist the thoughts, but rather *let go* of them. Let them float away. Every time they recur, do the same thing. Don't fight them.'

Words only acquire deeper significance against a backdrop of silence. We should talk less and listen more – especially to our Creator-Redeemer. His words resound through eternal silence. For the words that matter are not the words I am now writing, but those words God will speak in the silence of your heart.

Focused Prayer

Already I have referred to the stream of words and impressions that sweep across our minds continually. People who successfully learn about silence have learned how to detach themselves

from the stream. They tell us that to fight against
wandering thoughts is a frustrating waste of time.
You will never succeed in stopping that flow
of thoughts. Let them pursue their own merry
way! Some people tell us such thoughts are like
interesting boats drifting past us downstream.

If you find yourself climbing on one of the boats
out of interest, remember what your aim is. Let
them go, release them, and you may begin to
find that God is still there. William Kelly says,
'When you catch yourself again, lose no time in
self-recriminations, but breathe a silent prayer
for forgiveness and begin again, just where you
are. Offer *this* broken worship up to Him and say:
"This is what I am except Thou aid me." Admit no
discouragement, but ever return quietly to Him
and wait in His Presence.'9

A year or two ago I was walking in the early
morning beside a canal in the English country-
side. As I walked I happened to be in touch with
the silence and was communing with God. Then
something at the edge of the canal attracted my
attention, and I turned and stood staring at it.
A moment later, I remembered with shame that
I was supposed to be walking with God.

Instantly I turned and glanced at – at what?
For suddenly I was a tiny child, and the memory
of my earthly father came back. We had been
walking together when I was distracted by a
butterfly and squatted to examine it, absorbed
with wonder. Then, remembering Daddy, I turned
anxiously . . . to see him standing patiently, smiling as he waited. It was as though my heavenly
Father now stood waiting, smiling at his so easily
distracted child.

Patient persistence in turning back to him is

what prayer is about – day after day, week after week, month after month, year after year. But the rewards far exceed the cost. And it is in this way that most of my own sexuality has been sorted out.

Chapter 12

Healing Hidden Wounds Through the Body

Nor can a man with grace his soul inspire,
More than the candles set themselves on fire.
JOHN BUNYAN

By the grace of God (Dei gratia).
LATIN PHRASE

God yearns with fatherly yearning to heal you from your proclivity to sexual sin. He wants to make you like Christ. To do this he uses means to that end, means of grace. Already we have looked at two means of grace, repentance and prayer. In this chapter I want to look at the grace of God that the people of God have ministered to me. Such people were the *means*, the channel by which God's grace came to me. However, *you have to be willing to receive help from any source God offers*. You cannot afford to be choosy.

The Naaman Factor

Naaman had a lofty position. He was supreme commander of the Aramite forces (2 Kings 5). As such, he was accustomed to relating to people in a certain way. He commanded lesser beings. He understood the concept of hierarchy. He operated through channels and by protocol. Naaman also had a problem. He was a leper. And he was desperate for a cure. One source of help was to be found in Elisha, the prophet of Israel.

Israel at that time in Old Testament history was in decline, and Aram was a great nation. So Naaman would have to show great humility on two counts: first, for a commander to ask anyone for help, and second, for an Aramite to ask for help from an Israelite, someone from a nation he looked down on.

His pride was battered further when the prophet Elisha refused to see Naaman and merely sent a servant to speak to him. In addition, he was told by the servant to go and wash seven times in the miserable little Jordan River. It was unthinkable! The insults piled on insults incensed him.

The story is often used as children's Sunday-school material. It should really be material for adults, for Naaman's pride and rage are similar to our own. For me to descend from my psychiatric and ministerial pose was not, and is not, easy. To be sure, it was not only a pose. I really did have the kindest feelings toward patients, and also toward members of my congregation. I prayed frequently and individually with both – there in my office or after a church service. But my role was to counsel, to pray for others, to help others. I was a helper, not a 'help-ee.' I was comfortable in the role I understood. If I were to seek help, it would have to be from someone higher up in the hierarchy of helpers – and there were few people who qualified – or so I thought.

It never occurred to me that someone 'lower

on the scale' could minister to me. 'They' were
help*ees*, not help*ers*. My beliefs were orthodox: Of
course, the Holy Spirit could use anybody. But he
was very unlikely to! That is, I could not conceive
of his using younger, less experienced people to
help *me*.

It was a big mistake. I began to find that, while
experience certainly helps, God seems to be able
to use almost anybody. I needed to be humbled,
willing to receive help from any quarter, from
anybody a sovereign God chose to use for that
purpose. It was an enormous step, but a step that
is an investment paying rich dividends. I suspect
many of us who are counsellors or pastors need
to learn a lesson here. Ask yourself the question:
How comfortable would I be to receive spiritual
help from one of my clients – to have our roles
reversed?

The Church

The church, the body of Christ, was intended
among other things to be precisely a place where
anybody can help anybody. John Wimber speaks of
the church as being by turns a nursery for the newborn, a training and teaching institution, an army
in the battle with the powers of hell, and a hospital
for the wounded (whether the battle-wounded or
the damaged and wounded newborn). If the local
church is to become like this, then everybody in
the church has to be mobilised.

Few local churches function in all four areas.
Yet I believe all were meant to do so, and there
are signs that some churches may be doing so. One
reason for the failure of many churches to heal the
wounded is that, as we saw very early in the book,

many pastors are themselves involved in sexual
sin, as are many elders and deacons. In many such
churches no one wishes to bring the matter into
the open, and in others the church now proclaims
that certain forms of sexual sin are not sin at all.
Satan has been highly successful in making sexual
sin an inroad to other forms of sin!

Nevertheless, God's counter-offensive has begun.
I believe it may indicate the 'wave of the future.' A
greater degree of flexibility is returning to some of
our relationships in the church. Some help*ees* are
becoming occasional help*ers*.

God's People Who Minister Grace

God's grace is being ministered through his people
in the area of sexual (and other) sin. What are
you likely to encounter from such servants? How
do they go about what they do? One thing you
will certainly encounter is the area of 'split' and
forgotten memories as well as other issues already
reviewed.

At the moment, there is still a lack of workers
proportionate to the need. Their work is confined
to various conferences and courses. Some conferences are limited to sexuality. Others have a more
general approach, but one that includes sexuality.
Prominent among the emphases you will come
across as they pray for you will be the grace of God,
the place and significance of mental pictures, and
issues surrounding forgiveness. In this chapter
we will look at these emphases. Already we have
explored others.

These helpers may spend much longer praying
for you than you might be accustomed to. A healing
session may continue for three or four hours.

Where there is faith in God and a real sense
of his presence, his servants *want* to pray, want
to call on him for aid. Inquire when and where
such conferences are held. Seek out literature
describing methods of healing and sanctification.

(I list the names and addresses of agencies
willing to help you, as well as books you can
read, in the appendices at the back of the book.)

God's Exceeding Grace

John Bunyan tells us (in the quote that heads this
chapter) that you can no more produce the grace of
God by your own efforts than a candle could light
itself. He says this is in a book he wrote for children. Children understand grace, and they never
stop pleading for it from their parents. Grace is
what God gives you when you deserve nothing
but hell. Healing and sanctification come to us
by grace, even though we may be totally unaware
of that grace, attributing its effects to psychology
or whatever. Certainly you cannot inspire your
own soul with grace. God has to light your candle
for you.

Yet there *is* grace for you if you want and need it.
It has come to me along ways I have listed above,
including the recovery of sins of the past which I
had forgotten completely or whose real nature I
had never before seen. And God has similar ways
of dealing with sexual sins and occult practices
through his people.

A Personal Experience of a Traumatic Memory

One healing I experienced took the form of repentance. But it was a repentance that occurred while

others ministered to me. Two people were praying for me, a man and a woman. They told me that many others were praying – and I could tell. There was something about the whole time I spent with Dick and Anne (not their real names) that impressed me deeply. I saw them as more experienced than I in God's healing ways.

They spent quite a while allowing me to share my concerns with them, asking me questions from time to time. My concerns took the form of spiritual problems I struggled with. After a while we broke for coffee, then resumed after about fifteen minutes. They then anointed me with oil, not just because of the passage in James, but to remind us all of our dependence on the Holy Spirit. Immediately a couple of unusual things happened. First, the oil on my forehead produced a strong burning feeling.

'What on earth have you got in that stuff?' I asked.

They both smiled. Dick said, 'It's just common anointing oil. People react differently to it. Most people feel nothing. A few people complain as you have about burning, and one or two others develop a swelling where we mark a cross.' An allergic response? Perhaps. But I never felt a burning upon subsequent anointings with the same oil.

My second reaction was very significant. Over many years I have slowly learned to discern when an exceptional anointing of the Holy Spirit's power comes on me. One of the ways in which this happens is that I experience a weight, a sense of heaviness.[1] On that occasion, such was the weight that I could hardly move. I am *not* a suggestible person, and several attempts to hypnotise me during my psychiatric residency all failed. I have long since rejected hypnosis.

Immediately also, part of me became three years old while the rest of me remained adult. I cannot explain this, but it was very vivid. I became aware that when I was three I knew Jesus, not perhaps as Saviour, but as someone who took care of me and whom I loved. This surprised me. I had no idea of it and had forgotten completely. Yet immediately on the heels of the awareness came bitterness and anger. 'Why did you leave me?' the three-year-old part of me cried. 'Why did you go away?'

'Did he really go away, John?' Anne asked.

I seemed to be two people at the same time. At once the adult part saw that Jesus could not have abandoned me. *I* had turned my back on *him*. I had stopped trusting him, assuming he had left me. Aware of the fact that I must have grieved him, I began silently to weep. Before long I was telling him how sorry I was that I had grieved him, and was asking his forgiveness. I felt it keenly.

Forgiveness for the 'sin' of a child of three? Sin is sin, as deadly in a three-year-old as in an adult. Perhaps more deadly. In this respect it compares with cancer. Cancer is more virulent in young children. Let us be under no delusions about the deadliness of sin. Anything that occasioned the death of the Son of God must be horrendously dangerous. I experienced the forgiveness of God to me as I wept in repentance when the interview began.

Mental Pictures of God

As you seek sexual healing, you may encounter among evangelical Christians different approaches to 'seeing' things in your mind. First, let me point out that it is something we all do to some degree. We picture things. 'Yes, I can just see him doing that,' we may say. Or, 'You know, I see her face, but I don't seem to be able to recall her name just now.' Or, 'Yes, I know that street well. I can just picture it in my mind.'

Certainly God's people down the ages have seen some pretty vivid pictures. When John saw the risen Christ in Revelation 1 (before being invited 'up' in Rev 4:1), what was he seeing? *A vision*, you say. And what is a vision but 'seeing with the heart'? I know some visions are far more vivid than others, but all experiences of this kind represent a revelation to us of reality, of what is. But reality often has to be coded in a symbolic form. Raw reality is at times more than we can take. In any case, our natural eyes are not adapted to seeing spiritual realities.

When Elisha asked God to open the eyes of his servant, it was his heart's eyes that God opened (see 2 Kings 6:17–20). Our spiritual eyes need to be quickened by the Spirit of God, and then what we see can be seen with our physical eyes either open or shut.

The most dramatic 'seeings,' I find, come without our asking, totally unbidden. These one could see, I am sure, whether one's eyes were open or not. Mine have always been open when this has happened to me. I've never shut them to validate my theory, because I've been too overwhelmed by what (or whom) I see to worry about theories. But quieter and less obtrusive pictures are best perceived with eyes shut. All pictures are 'seeing with the heart' as it is quickened by the Spirit.

Instructing People to 'See' Jesus

'But we see Jesus,' says the writer to the Hebrews.
He also exhorts us with the words, 'looking unto
Jesus.' Is he not using metaphorical language?
Yes, of course. But where do metaphors come
from? How does a writer produce one? *He or
she sees a picture in the mind* and says, 'Yes,
that's it!' A picture elaborates itself so easily and
quickly that writers may not even be consciously
aware what of they are doing. Many of us do it
all the time. This is a God-created function which
God gave us when he created our brains, devoting
the right hemisphere to what we mistakenly call
intuitive processes. Those of us who are 'right-
brain' people will function more easily in this area,
while 'left-brainers' will tend to be more at home
with discursive logic.

I remind someone who has had a certain cruelty
or bewildering event take place in the past that
Christ by his Spirit was there. He is omnipresent,
always and everywhere present, whether perceived or not. This is reality. However, it is a
reality that surprises the people when they think
of the horrendous thing that happened to them.

Then I pray that God will enable the person
to see what Jesus did, or wanted to do, on that
occasion. I have been astounded again and again
at what happens. Solutions I could not have conceived become apparent. The Holy Spirit, who
alone knows the needs of each heart, ministers to
it according to its needs. Often the person weeps
for joy and wonder. I, for my part, realise over
again that my role in the whole affair is negligible,
that God and only God is doing the real work.

I have some misgivings about asking people to

see Jesus, because of some experiences I have had with people with an occultic background. It has not happened frequently, but the Jesus they see may not be Jesus at all.

The Struggle with Forgiveness

Earlier in the book we saw that many of our sexual struggles have their roots in confusion about our gender identity. The healing process includes this but, even more importantly, our sanctification as well. We see that forgiveness plays a critical role here, and that our own ability to forgive is related to how real God's forgiveness is to us.

I cannot exaggerate the importance of forgiveness toward those who have wronged us. You will find talk about it wherever people discuss healing. And when you encounter such talk you usually are standing on holy ground. Saving faith is faith of the heart, not just of the intellect. Demons believe – and tremble. Paul makes the matter plain: 'If you confess with your mouth, "Jesus is Lord," and believe in your heart that God raised him from the dead, you will be saved. For it is with your heart that you believe and are justified' (Rom 10:9–10).

Why my emphasis on heart? It is because Western education over-emphasises intellect, assuming that an intelligent grasp of something makes all the difference. Not so the Bible. B.O. Banwell notes:

The Hebrews thought in terms of subjective experience rather than objective scientific observation, and thereby avoided the modern error of over-departmentalization. It was

essentially the whole man, with all his attrib-
utes, physical, psychological and emotional,
of which the Hebrews thought and spoke,
and the heart was conceived of as the gov-
erning centre for all of these . . . There is no
suggestion in the Bible that the brain is the
centre of consciousness, thought or will. It is
the heart which is so regarded . . . It is the
heart that makes a man or a beast what he
is, and governs all his actions.[2]

Therefore, forgiveness must be heart-forgiveness;
the knowledge of forgiveness, a heart-knowledge;
and faith itself, heart faith. Such faith brings a
subjective awareness to the whole person. It is
my subjective awareness with every part of my
being that I am forgiven. Only the Holy Spirit can
impart such a knowledge of forgiveness. And as
we have already seen, it is such an experience of
being forgiven that makes a person's forgiveness
of others very much easier.

Leanne Payne mentions three barriers to the
healing, sanctifying process. They are failure to
forgive others, failure to receive forgiveness for
ourselves and failure to accept ourselves.[3] The
three are linked. The failure to forgive others and
the failure to receive forgiveness for ourselves are
clearly connected. As Jesus taught in the Lord's
Prayer, we are able to receive God's forgiveness to
the same degree to which we forgive others. Just
as an experience of being forgiven makes it easier
to forgive, so a lack of willingness to forgive may
be the cause of an absence of any sense of being
forgiven.

In addition, failure to accept ourselves cannot
be discussed properly unless it is based on an

awareness of my being forgiven and accepted by God. I begin to like myself when I know in my heart what God thinks about me.

Let me take the matter of giving forgiveness a step further. If you say, 'I'd like to forgive, but I just can't,' you stand on perilous ground, not on holy ground. What you may be saying is that to forgive is too painful. Up to now I have only discussed the amazing thing that happens when the Holy Spirit reveals to my heart God's forgiveness toward me. Suppose this has not ever taken place. Am I excused from forgiving because of the pain it causes me to forgive? Certainly not!

The pain of forgiving is no excuse. Sometimes forgiveness may have to begin with an exercise of the will. I may have to assert again and again, every time bitter feelings surge up in me, 'I *do*, I *will* forgive.' I must not give in to my pain, or I may never know God's loving, forgiving acceptance in my experience.

The Murder I Never Committed

As I waited on God one day, I began thinking about the man who once molested me. Then God's word came to me. 'Have you forgiven him?' he asked. 'You know that you must.'

'Sure. It's no problem. It doesn't mean anything to me now.'

Back came another word, 'How old would he be?'

'Oh – I don't know. I would guess at least ninety.'

Without any conscious intention, I began to picture him in my mind, sitting opposite me as he would be if he were still alive – bald, obese, a little

greasy, smiling coyly. Suddenly, aware of the man
I pictured, I was filled with rage. Everything that
I had pushed down below the level of awareness
rose up in me. My hands also rose up, reaching
for his neck to throttle him. Yet all this time I had
been convinced that I had forgiven him. *Obviously,
I had not forgiven.* It was just that I had put it
away from me into the distant past. I needed to
forgive him, and I did.

I forgave with my will. And I confessed my sin.
I resolved never again to allow any scorn of that
man to enter my mind. Many nights later I woke
thinking about the man again. Would I actually
have tried to strangle him if I had met him? Had
I forgiven him after all? I could imagine his face
reddening as I would have clutched his throat,
and as he tore at my hands to free himself. Then
I knew with absolute certainty that I could never
have followed through.

I recorded the whole thing in my journal the
next morning. As I did so, I saw that he was no
longer a threat to me. When I was a boy of eleven,
his manner, his laughing confidence, had overwhelmed me. His gentle mockery of my embarrassment and fear, my passivity, yet my inability
to go along with what he did had dumbfounded me.
Worse still, his ability to skillfully awaken erotic
feelings in me had awakened something else – disgust, hatred of him and hatred above all of myself.

Now I saw him differently. The old man I had
visualised (I doubt that he is alive; I have long
since lost track of him) was nothing like the
laughing, mocking memory of my boyhood. He
was a pathetic object. I experienced a profound
but gentle pity for his wretchedness. Forgive him?
How could I *not* forgive him?

The issue was resolved. It can be like this always. First comes the action of one's will. One decides to forgive, pain or no pain. One struggles against any thoughts that arise, any lack of a forgiving posture. Then, as the Holy Spirit continues to minister, there comes a resolution, a time when by one means or another all struggling ceases and the very need to struggle is gone. Thank God it is so.

Chapter 13

The Healing Session

> *But for you who revere my name, the sun of
> righteousness will rise with healing in its wings. And
> you will go out and leap like calves released from
> the stall.*
> MALACHI 4:2

> *Healing is simply the practical application of the
> basic Christian message of salvation, a belief that
> Jesus means to liberate us from personal sin and
> from emotional and physical sickness.*
> FRANCIS MACNUTT

Let us say that you have tried to prepare
yourself for the task of breaking the bondage
that sexual sin has over a person. Let us say that
you are as prepared as you know how to be. There
are one or two others with you, a small, prayerful
team of helpers. There is plenty of time to do what
you came to do. How do you start?

There is no set procedure, for we are to be led
by the Holy Spirit. The principal key to what you
will be doing is to hear what God is saying. It
is always good, however, to begin by uniting in
prayer in order to be in accord as a group, as
both those who minister and those who receive
ministry. And what better way to still our hearts

so that we can listen to the Spirit's voice? In prayer we invoke God's presence. He *is* present, but when we make it clear that we want him, acknowledge his presence, and start both to count on it and to praise him for it, we enter into partnership both with infinite power and infinite wisdom. At the same time we set our sails because to pray is also to listen and watch for the wind of the Spirit.

Collaboration on the Team

While one member should lead the group (whether it consists of only two persons or more than two), all should contribute. The working relationship of team members is crucial. They should know one another well, love one another, trust one another, have no hidden feelings of resentment toward one another. Therefore, they must pray together frequently and must keep short accounts with one another. Only in this way will they enjoy a good working relationship when they minister together.

Even so, tensions may arise during the course of the ministry. There may be a difference of opinion about the direction the Holy Spirit is leading. The leader should ask, from time to time, what other team members may have seen or heard from the Lord. Should the leader fail to do so, a member who is not leading may wish to suggest something. At a suitable moment the assistant may say, 'I think the Lord has been saying to me . . .' or, 'I keep getting the impression that . . .' or, 'I wonder if you would mind if I . . .'. The more people have worked together and the more mature they are as Christians, the more truly they love and trust one another, the better they will work as a unit under the direction of the Spirit.

Where to Begin

Many Christians begin by asserting their authority over the powers of darkness, demanding the departure of demonic presences. Already we have discussed this, and I have no objection to the practice, provided we do not thereby assume that all demons have obeyed. Remember also where our emphasis should lie. We are to focus on light more than on darkness, on Christ more than Satan, on angelic presences more than on the demonic.

But we should be cautions about doing this, or anything else by routine. Since demons make their appearances during the course of the ministry from time to time, it is clear that not all demons heed every order we may give. Christ's authority, even when it is rightly claimed by Christians, is at times resisted, even disputed. It can, therefore, be naive to assume that by means of a command we routinely give we can be sure of no demonic interference.

Nevertheless we do not back off. There can be value in stating the obvious aloud. We bear the authority of the king. The greatest value of such commands lies in declaring from the start where the authority lines are drawn. No darkness can continue to resist the authority of the King of Light indefinitely. It is important to remind ourselves that this is so. Too great a focus on the dark powers, on the other hand, is to be avoided.

Another place to start is with anointing with oil. This is a symbolic act with a long biblical history. Kings and priests were anointed (Ex 28:41, 1

Kings 19:15–16). James suggests that when elders are called, prayer for healing the sick be accompanied by anointing (Jas 5:14). The symbolism is that of the anointing by the Holy Spirit. The ideas are linked in Scripture. Saul's anointing for kingship was in fact followed very soon afterward by the Holy Spirit's anointing. 'Then Samuel took a flask of oil and poured it on Saul's head and kissed him, saying, "Has not the LORD anointed you leader over his inheritance?"' (1 Sam 10:1). And 'when they arrived at Gibeah, a procession of prophets met him; the Spirit of God came upon him in power, and he joined in their prophesying' (1 Sam 10:10).

It does not always happen like that, but, as mentioned in the last chapter, on one occasion in which I was anointed with oil (though it was the last thing I was expecting just then), the Holy Spirit came very heavily upon me. Still, there is nothing to say that anointing with oil is mandatory. Jesus never used oil when he healed people. In the vast majority of the healings of every variety that I have observed, oil has not been used. The practice is a biblical practice. It reminds us graphically of the need for, and our dependence on, the Holy Spirit's anointing, but must not itself become the centre or main focus.

The Healing Interview

What follows next would in most cases be a healing interview with the person being ministered to. John Wimber describes five essential steps.

Step 1: The Interview
Step 2: The Diagnostic Decision

Step 3: The Prayer Selection
Step 4: The Prayer Engagement
Step 5: Postprayer Directions[1]

Most experienced workers, while not always following the precise order that Wimber describes,
would accept that these five steps, as Wimber
describes them in the book *Power Healing*, are
essential. Some might add one or two more steps.
Let me deal first with the interview.

Step 1: The Interview

Unlike the situation in a large meeting or seminar,
time for taking a history is less of a problem when
you pray by appointment for a person. In spite
of this, you must take your time and resist the
temptation to hurry. Inner stillness is necessary
if we are to hear well.

We are all inclined to try to feel spiritual when
doing something 'Christian,' and to assume a posture of intensity. Many people are totally unaware
of the way they slip on their Christian Service
persona like a mask. Being spiritual and feeling
spiritual are not the same thing. To slow down, to
stop being artificially intense, to know what it is to
be still in God's presence commonly means we are
better able to focus on what God may be saying.
Intensity is usually carnal religiosity. It militates
against the Spirit's work.

Let us suppose we are trying to help a person
we will call Jerry. Having the time to do so,
we take advantage of it. We do not hurry. We
listen to Jerry, watching him carefully as we do
so. We watch his facial expressions, his bodily
movements. All the time we are trusting God to

speak, asking those questions that are prompted by what we observe or that the Spirit seems to suggest that we ask. The whole procedure should generally be quiet, tranquil. No hype, no pressure. Apart from any other consideration, this helps Jerry to be calm.

Our object is not to take a complete family and psychological history, so much as to sense the direction in which the Holy Spirit is leading. It is a procedure following heart and spirit rather than doing groundwork for an intellectual analysis of the problem. This is not to suggest that psychological insights we may already have should be ignored, or that we should shut off our brain function and not ask relevant questions. Rather our primary dependence will be on the Holy Spirit's leading. Wimber comments, 'I always have the attitude that it is easier to ask questions than think I must receive words of knowledge. But sometimes God reveals that what the person for whom I am praying thinks his or her need is, is not correct.'[2]

I shall certainly not triumph by means of an intellectual *tour de force*. Humble dependence on God, listening for his word, should characterize the whole procedure. However, we must not be fearful of asking personal questions of a delicate nature. The embarrassment will be halved if the questioner is not embarrassed. Your embarrassment, your awkwardness, awakens the same in people around you. The best way to ask a delicate question is to use few words and to ask it outright. Picture the following scenario:

You begin to speak by clearing your throat. Then, a little anxious, you mumble at the floor in a low voice, 'Do you, er, I mean, have you ever, like, 'um, mastur-'

Jerry says: 'I'm sorry. Could you speak up a little? I can't quite catch what you're saying.'

'Oh, I'm sorry. I mean – er . . .'

By this time you yourself will be more embarrassed than ever, even a little angry with yourself or with Jerry, so that everyone present will feel awkward. Be deliberate. Look Jerry in the eye and say firmly, clearly, and sympathetically, 'Has masturbation been a problem for you?' There is no need to apologise, or to elaborate by saying, for example, 'You know, I'm not accusing, only *asking* because it sometimes – er, d'you know?' When you say things like that you are giving way to your own insecurity. Your security comes not from your professional performance, but from trust in God. Experience, of course, brings tranquility, and you will lack experience when you begin. Therefore, be still before God. Be quiet in your spirit, but clear and simple in your speech.

Step 2: Diagnosis – The Problem's Root
The root meaning of the word *diagnosis* is 'to know through.' It is to be able to see through the surface to what lies beneath. The object you have in mind is to help someone with a problem, a problem that results in sin. You want to find why the sinful habit cannot be overcome, and to correct this. Very gently, but quite directly, you will ask about it, not focusing on the sin, but inquiring what steps have been taken to overcome it, what the person's ideas are of why it is not overcome, and what its roots are.

Jerry may not know the *why* of his problem. The problem itself looms so large that the very question has become a source of bitterness. He has racked his brains, has tortured himself relentlessly with the question why? Therefore, we must try to find the answer together. And since God is in the business of restoring people, we can be sure of his good will in the matter.

We must come to a conclusion, however, about the root of the problem. True, there may be several roots, so that more than one will have to be cut, but usually one is critical. It is at this point that God's willingness to speak is most important. The big question is whether we are listening.

The British and Canadian branches of Wholeness Through Christ, an organization that specialises in healing sexual sin, suggests four areas to keep in mind at this time – sins, emotional wounds and bondages, the occult, and heredity. It is not necessary to raise all four areas or to deal with each in turn. In any case there is a close interrelationship between them. Rather, as I continue to insist, we must allow God the Holy Spirit to lead us. To keep them in mind means that we are less likely to ignore a prompting from the Holy Spirit.

As you gain experience, you will discover how much there is to learn about each area. The more you do this sort of thing, the wider your experience becomes. Take the occult, for instance. I have already made my conviction clear that merely saying to demons we *believe* are there, 'I bind you in the name of Jesus,' does not mean the demon is necessarily bound. With some I find it to be a personal struggle.

Many differ about how you discern whether a demon is present. All are agreed that the Holy Spirit is the one who gives us illumination about the matter. But many Christians who believe

(sometimes mistakenly) that demons are present,
say, 'I bind you . . .' and then subsequently are not
surprised that no demonic manifestation occurs.
They assume that their experience confirms the
practice even though there is no evidence of such
a presence.

My own experience is of two kinds. In some
instances I sense God speaking and telling me
that a demon is present, even where there is no
apparent reason to suppose a demon might be
present. Yet as the Holy Spirit leads me to pray
for someone, the person suddenly grins and says,
'It's gone!' *even though neither of us had talked or
thought about demons until that moment.*

The other, and commoner experience, is for me
not even to be thinking about demons. I enter
a room, or else begin to pray for someone, or
begin to preach, and a demon manifests in a
noisy, dramatic fashion. Usually it responds to
my command to be silent or to quit doing whatever
it is doing, but occasionally there is a tussle of
wills. Once I had to give up, at least for the time
being. (I loathe dealing with demons.) The more I
experience, the more I realise how little I know.
All I know is that I have authority to cast them
out, am commanded to do so, and must obey the
word of the living God.

Some of my acquaintances, who seem more
sure of their ground than I do, say, 'We know
our command to bind the demon works because
we never get the sort of manifestations you get.'
Remember, I am referring to a *routine* use of
binding (or similar) commands, when there is no
particular evidence of their presence. Recently I
remembered an old elephant joke. It had to do with
the man who walked round constantly snapping

his fingers. When asked why he did so, he replied, 'To keep elephants away.'

His friend objected, 'But there *are* no elephants around here,' only to be told, 'No. Of course not. See how well it works.'

During the years I have been dealing with demonised people I have realised that no two demons are the same, no two demonised persons are alike. What worked with one will not necessarily work with another. There are few set rules. The issue with authority is a non-issue. We have authority. I am reduced to two basic principles at the moment, principles which apply to every case I have come across.

One I have been insisting on – the importance of hearing the voice of the Spirit. When *he* says 'Do this or that,' it is the right thing to do. The other is that I must focus more on the person I am helping than on the demon I am expelling. You don't get involved with, argue with, or allow yourself to be fascinated by the demonic performance. Instead, you command it to quit or to be silent. So I say (in effect), 'In Jesus' name, shut up! I'm talking to Susan. Susan, can you hear me?' But always I crave the Spirit's voice. Casting out a demon affects three beings – yourself, the victim and the demon. Only God knows all three of you, and that intimately. Only he can see the best strategy. Hence the importance of hearing his voice.

I have discussed the occult to emphasise that all four areas I mentioned are ever-expanding areas. The further we go, the more we discover about the occult, about blood lines, about sin, and about wounds and bondages. We cannot learn them from books any more than we can learn the sufficiency of Christ from books. And if we could, we probably would not use them to the best advantage because we would be relying on our knowledge rather than on the Lord himself. We would tend to think we knew enough – and none of us ever does.

Steps 3 and 4: The Prayer Selection and Engagement
I shall never tire of repeating that prayer begins with God, not with us. We pray effectively when our prayer coincides with the will of God. We know that will in general through Scripture, but Scripture does not cover every situation. Scripture does not reveal to me the thing that Jerry is trying to conceal. Only the voice of the Spirit is of help here. And even when I know what Jerry is hiding, and have told him so, I may still not know the best way of resolving the issue. In the same way, Wimber says, 'I always ask God how I should pray for a sick person . . . even when I have a clear understanding of the cause of a condition, I am not sure about how to pray specifically.'[3]

He gives several examples of this, talking about *words of command, words of pronouncement, words of rebuke,* all uttered in the context of prayer.[4] It is unwise to assume we always know how to pray. Last night, for instance, some of us were praying for an older married missionary couple. As I prayed for the man I sensed that very real but unknown physical danger lay ahead of him. The time of danger was in the future – perhaps a year or two away. Alarmed, indeed a little frightened, I pleaded with God for him, asking for mercy and protection. Meanwhile my wife, Lorrie, was sitting quietly on the floor and had opened her Bible. As, still bothered, I concluded my prayer, Lorrie said to the man, 'I *think* God has given me this psalm for you.'

Relief flooded through me as she began to read to him:

He will not let your foot slip –
he who watches over you will not slumber . . .
The LORD watches over you –
The LORD is your shade at your right hand;
the sun will not harm you by day,
nor the moon by night.
The LORD will keep you from all harm –
he will watch over your life. (Ps 121:3–7)

Afterward she told me, 'While you were praying, God told me to open my Bible. He didn't tell me *where* to open it, just to open it – so I did. Then, when I heard your concern about danger, I happened to glance down at my Bible, and immediately I saw Psalm 121. As I read it I knew I had to read it aloud.'

All during my own prayer I had been pausing to look to God and had proceeded with each sentence only as I sensed how God was leading. I was not altogether satisfied with the lack of resolution at the end. Lorrie had in the same way been listening. All she had done was obey the word of the Lord. It was all she had to do. Whether we will ever learn what the danger is and what happens, I do not know.

Lorrie did not have any set procedure. She heard and obeyed. It is not that set procedures are wrong, but they must never become the only means to the end in view. The channels of healing are so many, and God commonly knows how he wants to heal.

This morning I was talking on the telephone to

a friend, Henry, who hears from God clearly. He
described how a younger Christian, Al, had come
into the room where several others were standing. Al had just finished ministering in public
and began to talk, anxious (though he never
said so) to know what everyone thought of his
performance. He was fishing for reassurance from
more experienced colleagues.

Perceiving this, and knowing that what people
think about us never satisfies, Henry silently
asked God what to do — essentially what sort
of prayer to pray. 'Go kneel in front of him,
place his hands together between your own, and
ask me to tell Al what *I* think of what he did.'
Henry followed the instruction carefully and then
prayed. Within seconds the look of eager anxiety
on Al's face drained away, replaced by gratitude
and awe. 'He told me he gave me an A+!' Al said
wonderingly.

How would you have responded to a man fishing
for reassurance, hoping for compliments? You
could say, 'Al, you did great!' Or knowing his
real need, you could say, 'You did very well. But
you know, your need is to look to God rather than
to the rest of us. Why don't we pray together,
confessing this to God, and ask him to help you
be independent of what the rest of us think.'
Instead, Henry asked God how to pray. What
God told Al both taught him a lesson, and gave
him a peace which no amount of compliments
could have brought.

Engaging in prayer can (though it need not be)
accompanied by many forms of physical manifestation. Once Lorrie and I were praying for a lady
who was severely ill, and who 'didn't believe in
that sort of thing.' Nevertheless, she had agreed

to let us try. As we prayed, she said, 'Oh! My arms and legs want to move about.'

We said, 'Well, let them!' A series of flailings and jerks followed.

Suddenly the woman began to weep, crying out after a moment, 'It's all right, H—, I forgive you! It doesn't matter any more!' We never found out what H— had done. What was obvious was that the Lord had convicted her of an unforgiving attitude, of harbouring resentment against someone who had wronged her. When she rose to leave us, she had been healed of a major physical illness.

I do not commonly see such manifestations when I pray, and they occur mostly when I pray for a physical illness, or for the demonised. When I pray for an emotional condition, weeping is more common.

One man for whom I prayed had cancer. He began to shake, and the shaking became so bad we had to sit him down. It was the first time that this sort of thing had happened to me, and I was awed and excited. I followed my usual practice of listening after each phrase, trying to pray only as the Spirit led. With each phrase it was as though jolts of electricity went through him. Finally he jumped to his feet, crying, 'It's done! It's finished!' A large, hard abdominal mass had disappeared, gone.

But something inside me said, 'No! It's not finished.' However, we terminated the meeting. I laid aside my doubts, excited by what had already taken place. A few years later the cancer returned, ending his life.[5]

Step 5: Postprayer Directions (Follow-up)
Even when there is a dramatic manifestation of

the Holy Spirit's intervention, that is not what matters. The key is that the person walk by faith, not by whatever experiences he or she may or may not have had. With the passage of time, memories fade, and with fading memories, the vividness of a particular encounter with God grows too evanescent to count on. You say to yourself, 'Did that really happen? Or was it all in my head? Maybe I'm remembering it wrongly. In any case it could be just psychological.'

Wholeness Through Christ members talk about 'walking out your healing.' They emphasise walking by faith, putting on the armour of God, memorizing God's promises in Scripture. It is in the name and character of God that our faith is rooted, in someone who loves us and never mocks us, whose written word is solid as a rock.

Where we are dealing with sexual sin, it is always essential to warn against repeating old sins. The sense of freedom one has at first, and the fading from memory of past events makes it easy for the enemy to tell us a year or two later, 'Once will not cause too much damage. You've been under stress. It's not *that* bad. Give way for once.'

At that point we need to hear again the words of Jesus, 'Go, and sin no more!' I have found from personal experience that deliverance a second time will be far harder than the first time. We should not, like the sow, return to the mire, or like the dog to our own vomit. To do so is to despise Christ's awful darkness and death. And where physical healing is concerned (as I mention in note 5), the consequences can be fatal. When he healed the man at the Pool of Bethesda,

Jesus reacted as he did on another occasion. 'Later Jesus found him at the temple and said to him, "See, you are well again. Stop sinning *or something worse may happen to you*"' (my italics, Jn 5:14).

Chapter 14

Your Future

*But God chose the foolish things of the world to
shame the wise; God chose the weak things of the
world to shame the strong. He chose the lowly things
of this world and the despised things – and the
things that are not – to nullify the things that are, so
that no-one may boast before him.*
1 CORINTHIANS 1:27–29

P aul the apostle had a weakness, an 'infirmity.'
In 2 Corinthians 12:7–10, he says God *gave*
him that weakness, yet he calls it 'a messenger of
Satan, to torment me.' It came from Satan, yet
God sent it.

Glorying in Your Weakness

Many arguments have arisen about the nature of
that weakness. Some people feel it was a sickness,
others that it had to do with the opposition and
persecution he faced. My own feeling is that it may
have had more to do with the way he handled the
opposition (certainly he talks about his weakness
in the context of the opposition from the Judaizing
party in the early church). Judging by some of his
comments in the second Corinthian epistle, he was
pretty touchy about their criticisms. However, the

precise nature of the 'infirmity' is neither here nor there.

Then what is the point in his mentioning it? It is the *purpose* of the weakness that matters, not its nature. Its purpose was to 'keep me from becoming conceited.' God allowed a weakness to remain in Paul's life, *to keep him from feeling he had 'had it made.'* That is why I think it may have had to do with how he handled criticism and opposition. He may well have struggled against what we now call defensiveness, resentment, bitterness in the face of the Judaizing party's attacks on him. Defensiveness, resentment and bitterness are satanic in their origin. They are certainly messengers of Satan.

But no matter. Paul was aware of a weakness, a weakness he did not want, yet a weakness *about which he begins to boast*. 'Therefore I will boast all the more gladly about my weaknesses, so that Christ's power may rest on me' (2 Cor 12:9).

There are two astonishing aspects to his statement. The first has to do with the relationship between strength and weakness; the second, the idea of actually boasting about a weakness. Let me deal with the second aspect first. The principle Paul talks about is a universal principle, and one that holds good in the case of sexual sins and weaknesses.

Take, for example, the most looked-down-on sexual sin and weakness of all, that of molesting little children. Even if you never gave way to it (many people cannot help themselves), if you found yourself tempted by it from time to time, you would never want to admit the temptation, much less to 'glory in' such a character flaw. Weaknesses

like that make us ashamed. Yet Paul finds in
his weakness a glorying, a boasting, a secret of
extraordinary power. It releases the power of
the Christ whose strength is made perfect in
weakness.

As we return to the relation of strength and
weakness, let us imagine, for a moment, what
it would feel like to know deliverance from the
weakness of molesting children. How would you
feel when you were delivered?

I can tell you from my experience of similar deliverances that you would be overwhelmed.
You would want to tell people about it. However, that phase might pass fairly soon. Among
the changes you would experience would be the
gradual assumption that you no longer had any
weakness in that direction. Then a day would
come when you felt the pull of temptation again.
A messenger of Satan would begin to torment you.
Messengers of Satan act like worms of death and
corruption working inside you. You would cry,
'Why, Lord? Why?' You would wonder what had
gone wrong.

You had not realised that Christ's strength is
made perfect not in your strength but in your
weakness. You had assumed that the strength
of your deliverance belonged to you *independent
of Christ*. It does not. The strength lies in a
relationship, in your dependent relationship with
him. It is a relationship of trust. The relationship
was strengthened at the moment of your greatest weakness – when he delivered you. Feeling
your weakness again calls you back to the place
where you recognise your weakness, where you
hit bottom again and cry out to Christ. Therefore,
come to him again and again. It is the only way

to keep yourself free from the crawling worms of death.

Accountability

Old habits die hard. The enemy will not leave us alone instantly. Long experience has taught us that we all need one another in the body of Christ. We need someone to be accountable to. It is all very well to assert that we trust in God alone. God has placed us within a body of believers so that we may confess to one another and pray for one another.

You must determine right away that you will, God helping you, find a person who will hold you accountable. It must not be someone with whom you can fall into sin. And it must be a person who really will hold you accountable and will take his or her task seriously.

I have a friend who was once a victim of satyriasis (a word used to describe a man with an insatiable appetite for women). He was known on occasion to use six prostitutes in one day. His enslaving drive to copulate ended his two marriages. He was also a pastor, and his problem (rightly) lost him his churches. God, in mercy, intervened in his life to heal and sanctify him.

God also provided him with a man to whom he was accountable. In his case it was an ideal mentor – a man with insight, who always seemed to know when he began to slip, as he did occasionally. One day his mentor suggested that they drive around to all the places where previous dalliances had occurred. In each place my friend tore down through prayer the 'altar to Baal' that he had erected there, and built one to the Lord, his God.

What the Holy Spirit had begun a year or two
before was completed that day.

Find someone who will hold you accountable.
And be honest with that person.

Your New Calling

If, as you have been reading, you have found
yourself saying, 'I needed this book,' pause for
a moment. God has more in mind than just you.
He is also thinking of and longing for many others
like you. He desires not only to heal (that is, to
sanctify) you, but to reach other victims of the old
fertility gods through you. Not through this book.
Through *you*.

'Oh, no, not through me!' you may say, but I
am perfectly serious. What you must grasp is
that the weakness in which Paul gloried made
him the greatest of all missionary pioneers. God
specialises in using the wounded and the broken
to heal others. True, your own healing must begin
first. But once it begins, God will draw other men
and women to you, other wounded who need
healing. You are being healed that you might
heal them. Your effective service for God is not
ending. Your real usefulness is about to begin.

You may be able to create a fellowship group
for other strugglers within your church. Together
you can covenant to share both triumphs and
failures with one another. Together you can pray
and minister Christ to one another.

The Importance of Being a Loser

So concerned is God that no flesh should glory in
his presence, that his policy throughout history
has been one of showing extreme preference for

the weak, the wounded, the defeated, the losers, people of no account, the outcasts of the earth. Not only so, they are his favourite soldiers, specially selected as his workers, his army, those who are to do his bidding.

Jesus chose a very odd group of apostles upon which to found the church. They were hardly the cream of religious society. None of them would have been chosen 'most likely to succeed.' They were, at best, the petit bourgeois of their day. Some of the disciples and the women had a distinctly less salubrious background. One woman dear to the Lord had been a prostitute. But she was forgiven and made whole by and in her relationship with Christ. Therefore, she washed his feet with her tears of gratitude, wiping them with the hairs of her head. Of such is the kingdom of God.

On the other hand, when we want help we prefer that the help be competent, well trained. But the trouble with the well trained is that eventually they may rely on their training rather than on God. Latent within every one of us lies the spirit of phariseeism. Well-trained people are in special danger. They have not always known a sense of desperation and may therefore lack an overwhelming sense of gratitude.

In addition, they are inclined to enjoy the perks that come to the well trained. It is so hard to be highly respected without beginning to respect yourself just a little! I know – I've been there. You gradually forfeit your capacity to sympathise with the world's losers. You fail to see your own weaknesses clearly, and you fail to have the kind of gut-wrenching compassion that Jesus experienced for hurting, sinful people.

In this way the well educated, many of whose

grandparents and great-grandparents struggled out of poverty themselves, come under the judgement of the God who brings down the proud and exalts those of low degree.

> Brothers, think of what you were when you were called. Not many of you were wise by human standards; not many were influential; not many were of noble birth. But God chose the foolish things of the world to shame the wise; God chose the weak things of the world to shame the strong. He chose the lowly things of this world and the despised things – and the things that are not – to nullify the things that are, so that no-one may boast before him.
>
> (1 Cor 1:26–29)

Yet the training itself is valuable. We need theologians and Bible scholars. We need trained and experienced counsellors. It is false expectations about training we must beware of.

All healers of others are wounded healers – whether or not we recognise the fact. Healers who know they are wounded are the most effective. But notice my qualification. You must never forget either those wounds that have been healed, or the wounds by which they were healed.

Remembering both kinds of wounds, you who struggle against sexual sin must, as you begin to be healed, also begin to help others. At first you will not be able to help much, but the help you can give will grow. Never allow yourself to be overconfident. Get all the training you can, though your own healing will be the most significant factor in your training. But never run away from the reality of those means of grace by which healing will come to you. Over and over again I must emphasise the importance of getting back to the beginning, of remembering the basics.

Blessed Were the Pharisees

Pharisees are people who know, people who are 'in the know,' who share a common 'in' language. As such they typify many well-trained people, whether the theologically well trained or the trained counsellors of various disciplines. Knowledge 'puffeth up.' It turns some people into balloons, into wordy bags of gas.

The Pharisees may well have begun as faithful servants of God more than two hundred years before Christ. During the reign of the tyrannical Antiochus IV, many Jews chose to risk their lives for their belief in Moses and to study the Scriptures all the more. God honours such men and women. Yet two hundred years later the Pharisees – spiritual descendants of men whom God must have honoured – received withering condemnation from Jesus. It is not by any means an unbreakable rule, but it often happens that the grandchildren of today's saints become tomorrow's Pharisees.

Do not become like them. A little knowledge is said to be a dangerous thing. But it becomes a dangerous thing only at the point where we start to overestimate ourselves, where our confidence no longer lies in the Son of God but in how much we know about him. At that point we forget what it was like to be a loser, and we become overconfident and proud. Never forget the bitter pains and struggles of the past. Never forget the times when you hated yourself, when you were

in the depths of despair. For the latent spirit of
phariseeism lies within all of us, professionals
and nonprofessionals, scholars and rank amateurs, theologians and brand new Bible readers,
wounded or healed.

Remaining Vulnerable

This morning I had a strange but very wonderful
experience as I sought God in prayer. For two or
three days, in spite of all our care not to take
on too many responsibilities, Lorrie and I have
experienced one pressure after another. Then this
morning at two a.m., a police officer called at our
door asking whether we were willing to accept a
man who had stayed with us previously and who
was now 'very intoxicated.' He had been knocking
on people's doors in a confused state.

I need not go into the man's history, except to
say that he also had a number of sexual problems.
Suffice it to say that being dragged to the door by
the police at two a.m. seemed the last straw in a
series of needless pressures. The timing was all
wrong. What was a sovereign God thinking about?
The pressure on my wife and myself was almost
unbearable.

The officer asked, 'Are you willing to receive
him?' It was a full minute before I said, 'Yes,
okay.' I was only half-awake and not thinking very
clearly. Lorrie was up by then and said, 'Put him
in my study, John.' It was the one place we could
use, for Lorrie had two women's Bible studies the
next day, one of them with nearly forty women –
and we already had three house guests.

The drunk man wanted to talk, and neither of
us was in a talking mood. We got him to bed –

and then, without thinking of Lorrie, I went to bed myself. I was dog tired, yet I did not sleep. Then I remembered Lorrie's Bible studies. She would need every opportunity for quiet tomorrow, and I had brought in a drunk. She had still not returned to bed. So I got up, went back to where she sat in the den in her favourite chair, almost too weary to move. I prayed with her. Then I kept her company until she herself said, 'Let's go back to bed.'

In the morning I felt dreadful, waking much later than usual and having no time to shave, shower or spend an adequate amount of time with God. I knew that the reduced prayer time mattered less than at one time I would have thought. Still, I craved what I could not have. I was in a foul mood, tired, selfish, self-pitying. I questioned my motives for admitting the drunk the previous night. I had added to Lorrie's already full programme. Did I really care for my wife? Was I a mere legalist, just doing the 'spiritual thing'? I allowed cynical thoughts to dominate me.

In that sort of mood I start to think raw sex. I've no idea why – except that it fits in with a mood of general disgust with life. I didn't care. Whether I had a right to or not, I enjoyed my foul and sexy mood. And then the Holy Spirit said quietly, 'Go ahead. Complain! Tell me I'm not playing fair, if that's what you think.' He was not being indifferent, but genuinely kind. He would have heeded my complaints and answered me.

Instead I realised what a louse I was, how weak, how cowardly and what a fool. At first the awareness brought me no comfort, at least until a new awareness began to dawn. I was a loser. Losers were the very kind of people Jesus received. The fact that I knew myself, that I

accepted my loser status meant *that he would
not reject me*. Then it happened. Light flooded my
night, turning it into day. Profound joy burst out
of my heart. 'Here I am, Lord! I need you! I'm the
worst sort of weakling, yet I know you will receive
me. Here I come!'

How can I explain what happened? The whole
day has been glorious. I sit here at my computer,
itchy, unshaven . . . but joyful. I was vulnerable.
I knew and accepted my weakness. I came again
to my Saviour, aware of my need of him, knowing
deeply how glad he would be to receive me. Mine
was the same sort of awareness of weakness about
which Paul talked in the passage that opened this
chapter.

To 'hit bottom' is an Alcoholics Anonymous (AA)
term describing what happened to me. It is the
same thing that I described of Augustine in a
previous chapter. But it is not to be a once-in-a-
lifetime event. God desires to bring us to that place
again and again, not to humiliate us, but because
the awareness of our hopelessness releases his
power within us. It is to be an ongoing experience,
the prelude to a new phase in the sanctifying
journey, a new empowering.

Turning Victims into Rescuers

I take my hat off to AA. It is not that their ideas
are perfect. (They are accused of weakening and
toning down the gospel.) The supreme value of
AA is that they turn victims of alcoholism into
rescuers. Nobody is more enthused to reach others
than an AA member who, having 'reached bottom'
and seen his or her helplessness, reaches out and
discovers there's Someone there.

This is why I salute them. They do more. They minister to, among others, the kind of people who cannot afford to attend expensive programmes. They are a volunteer movement, a movement of amateurs helping future amateurs, a movement for recycling survivors to make them rescuers. That is precisely what Jesus did with the twelve apostles and with the seventy-two disciples as well. Through them he changed the first-century world.

In the same way, Exodus International (one or two of whose chapters used to be called Homosexuals Anonymous) turns former homosexuals into men and women who minister to other homosexuals who are seeking a new way of life. Whatever the nature of your sexual problem, and however messed up your life may have been, God wishes to use the very weakness that once ruined you as your most effective area of usefulness. Your weakness can become your greatest strength, the source of your greatest usefulness to God and to your fellow men and women.

The Blessed Ones

Those who will inherit the earth, its future lords, will be ex-losers (Mt 5:5). Knowing and accepting that they are losers, they will find God's answer. It is faith in the power of Christ that turns losers into lords. In the beatitudes Jesus teaches this principle.

The poor in spirit, whom Jesus calls blessed (Mt 5:3), are those people who know they have nothing of value to offer to God except their poor, defeated, weak and worthless selves. They may come from the world's aristocracy, have studied

at the best schools and lived in Europe, be fluent
in five modern languages as well as in Latin,
Greek and Hebrew, yet still be of no value to
the kingdom. Only when we are weighed in the
divine balance and really see by how much we are
found wanting can other things become valuable.
The gifts are useful – but they are no credit to
us because they were given to us by God. *In our
rebellion and sin we are of no worth*, and this
fact renders all our talents and achievements as
wood, hay and stubble, ready for burning. Paul
counted them refuse compared to the excellency
of knowing Christ.

Therefore, if your sexual sins and weaknesses
make you feel horrible – rejoice! Accept what you
are and lay yourself at the feet of the Christ who
longs to receive you. Your value lies in the fact
that he made you and now longs to redeem you.
For in knowing your poverty you begin to fit every
category of people the Sermon on the Mount
describes. You will mourn and be comforted, be
meek and inherit the earth, hunger and thirst for
righteousness and be filled. Out of weakness you
will be made strong. You will put to flight the
powers of darkness.

So rejoice! An unbelievably glorious future lies
ahead of you. You are to become the salt of the
earth, a powerful preservative in the putrefying
society of which you are a part. You will be joining
the ranks of the soldier-saints who do not count
their lives dear to themselves, who will be valiant
in faith. Your wounds are there to be healed. Your
strength lies in your weakness itself, your glory in
the One who washes away your shame.

A distant trumpet is blowing. Listen carefully.
Can you hear it? It calls you by name. A voice

sounds. It calls you by name. A kingdom of glorious power has dawned among us, and you are personally invited to join. You are to be part of an invincible force. Nothing in earth or hell can stop it. No longer is a mere archangel like Michael to lead us, but the King of Glory himself. Your leader is Captain of the hosts of light. His ways are inscrutable and his purposes are unstoppable.

Dawn has broken and the Son will soon arise. Lift up your head! Don't let your hands hang down a moment longer! Quicken your pace! You are about to trample your enemies under your feet.

Appendix A: Organisations to Help You

UK Christian agencies dealing specifically with gender identity and sexual issues:

Living Waters UK
PO Box 1530
London SW1W 0GW

Local church-based discipleship programme with special emphasis on gender identity and sexual issues, including homosexuality.

Wholeness Through Christ
11 Arthur Street
Oswestry
Shropshire SY11 1JN

Specialises in healing prayer for leaders.

Overseas agencies:

Pastoral Care Ministries (President Leanne Payne)
PO Box 1313
Wheaton
Illinois 60189–1313
USA

Desert Stream Ministries (Director Andy Comiskey)
1415 Santa Monica Mall
Suite 201
Santa Monica
California 90401
USA

Exodus International
PO Box 2121
San Rufael
California 94912
USA

Vineyard Ministries International
PO Box 65004
Anaheim
California 92805
USA

UK Christian agencies dealing solely with the issue of homosexuality:

Courage
PO Box 338
Watford WD1 4BQ   Tel: 0181–420 1066

Residential programme with regular teaching to help people overcome homosexuality.

Pilot Trust
116 Shankill Road
Belfast BT13 2BD   Tel: 01232 230743

True Freedom Trust
PO Box 592
London SE4 1EF   Tel: 0181–314 5735

Biblically based counselling support groups, teaching
seminars and literature on homosexuality and related
problems.

U-Turn Anglia Trust
PO Box 138
Ipswich
Suffolk IP4 4RY   Tel: 01473 716121

Christian counselling ministry to homosexual men
and women seeking healing; assisting church understanding.

Appendix B: Books to Get You Started

The following books do not represent a comprehensive reading list but constitute a suggested place to begin in three areas *Set Free!* has dealt with: (1) manhood, womanhood and marriage; (2) general sexual healing; and (3) spirituality and prayer.

Books About Manhood, Womanhood and Marriage

Robert Bly. *Iron John*. New York: Vintage Books, 1992.

Gordon Dalby. *Healing the Masculine Soul*. Dallas: Word Publishing, 1988.

James G Friesen. *Uncovering the Mystery of MPD*. San Bernardino, Calif.: Here's Life Publishers, 1991.

Sam Keen. *Fire in the Belly*. New York: Bantam Books, 1992.

Kevin Marron. *Ritual Abuse: Canada's Most Infamous Trial on Child Abuse*. Toronto: McClellan-Bantam Seal Books, 1989.

Mike Mason. *The Mystery of Marriage*. Portland, Ore.: Multnomah Press, 1985.

John Piper and Wayne Grudem, eds. *Recovering Biblical Manhood and Womanhood*. Wheaton, Ill.: Crossway Books, 1991. Although this book is addressed to biblical scholars, the preface, foreword and first section are not technical and would repay perusal by people not versed in biblical scholarship.

Books About General and Sexual Healing
The following do not include psychiatric texts.

Elizabeth Moberly. *Homosexuality: A New Christian Ethic*. Cambridge: James Clark and Co., 1983.

Leanne Payne. *The Broken Image*. Eastbourne: Kingsway, 1988.

Leanne Payne. *Crisis in Masculinity*. Eastbourne: Kingsway 1988.

Leanne Payne. *The Healing Presence*. Eastbourne: Kingsway 1990.

David A. Seamands. *Healing of Memories*. Amersham: Scripture Press, 1986.

John White. *Eros Redeemed*. Guildford: Eagle, 1994.

Books About Spirituality and Prayer
Books about spirituality vary in their underlying theology. Their aim is usually more practical – to teach methods by which one is better able to hear God's voice. However, no one method fits everybody, and each of us eventually finds how best to do so.

Anthony Bloom. *Beginning to Pray*. New York: Paulist Press, 1970. (Published in Britain by Darton, Longman and Todd, Ltd., under the title *School for Prayer*.)

Richard Foster. *Prayer*. London: Hodder and Stoughton. 1992.

Joyce Huggett. *Listening to God*. London: Hodder and Stoughton, 1986.

Thomas S. Keating. *Open Mind, Open Heart*. Element Shaftesbury, 1991.

Brother Lawrence (Frank Laubach, ed.). *Practising the Presence*. Auburn, Maine: Christian Books, 1973.

Henri Nouwen. *The Way of the Heart*. London: Daybreak, 1990.

Notes

Chapter 1: A Sin-Stained Church in a Sex-Sated Society

[1] How Common Is Pastoral Indiscretion? *Leadership* 9, no 1 (Winter, 1988), p 12.
[2] Francis Frangipane, *The Three Battlegrounds* (Marion, Iowa: Frangipane, 1989), p 100.
[3] For a further treatment, see John White, *Changing on the Inside: The Keys to Spiritual Recovery and Lasting Change* (Guildford: Eagle, 1991).

Chapter 2: Overcoming Sexual Sin

[1] I do not say *the* way, but *one* way, perhaps the most important way. However, virginal men and women throughout history have been able to enter into exquisitely intimate fellowship with God. Clearly, sex is not the only way.

Chapter 3: Sexual Sin and Violence

[1] 'Confronting the Social Deficit,' *U.S. News and World Report*, February 8, 1993, p 28.
[2] Joseph J. Senna and Larry J. Siegal, *Introduction to Criminal Justice* (Minneapolis: West, 1993), pp 55–59.
[3] Ibid., p 57.
[4] Ibid., p 58.
[5] Report no. 35 of the Department of Peace and Conflict Research of Upsalla University. A statement in the preface by Peter Wallenstein, professor and head of the department.

Chapter 4: Satanic Sex

1 Bob and Gretchen Passantino, 'Hard Facts About Satanic Ritual Abuse,' *Christian Research Journal*, Winter 1992, pp 20ff.

2 See Susan J. Kelly, 'Ritualistic Abuse in Children,' *Cultic Studies Journal* 5: 228ff. See also Judith Spencer, *Suffer the Child* (New York: Simon and Schuster, 1989). This story cannot be verified, since names and other details have been changed to protect the individuals concerned from reprisals.

3 Ken Blue, formerly the pastor of the Delta Vineyard in our area is currently a pastor in Southern California.

4 When I speak of a demonic manifestation, I refer to a sudden eruption of a dramatic change in the person's behaviour. It may take the form of an outbreak of cursing the name of God or Christ, of writhing like a snake and hissing, of an epileptiform seizure, of feats of extraordinary strength or agility, or even of levitation. I have never seen the latter, but have witnessed all the others I mention, commonly in response to my own preaching, to my approaching someone or to my praying for someone.

Chapter 5: The Marriage of Sex and Love

1 C.S. Lewis, *The Four Loves* (Glasgow: Collins/Fount, 1989), p 14.

2 The words *'in pursuit of an orgasm'* are important. Sometimes men and women who have developed an unwholesome fear of sexuality or of their own bodies are advised to explore their body's sensations. They are counselled in particular to explore their erotogenic areas and not to be afraid of arousing them.

 I would add a caution. If the advice is an open invitation to masturbation, it is unfortunate. There is a fine line between *discovery* of the pleasures of the body and the *pursuit* of those pleasures. To pursue them for their own sake is to make an idol of them.

3 Thomas R. Kelly, *A Testament of Devotion* (New York: Harper & Row, 1941, n.e. 1992), p 62.

4 Ibid., p 39.

Chapter 6: Sex and Gender Confusion

1 Karl Stern, *The Flight from Woman* (New York: Farrar, Staus and Giroux, 1965), p 39.
2 The search for male identity is evidenced by the modern men's movement and by such recent books as sociologist Sam Keen's *Fire in the Belly: On Being a Man*, poet Robert Bly's *Iron John* and Gordon Dalbey's *Healing the Masculine Soul*.
3 John Owen makes that issue clear. He talks about the *grace of union*, meaning the union of divine and human natures in Christ, pointing out that 'the uniting of the natures of God and man in one person made him fit to be a Saviour to the uttermost. He lays his hand upon God, by partaking of his nature, Zech xiii 7; and he lays his hand upon us, by being partaker of our nature, Heb ii 14, 16: and so becomes a days-man, or umpire between both.' *The Works of John Owen* (London: Banner of Truth Trust, 1965), 2:51.
4 Leanne Payne, *Crisis in Masculinity* (Eastbourne: Kingsway, 1988), p 49.

Chapter 7: The Roots of Inversion

1 John White, *Eros Defiled* (Leicester: InterVarsity Press, 1978). See chapter six, pp 105–39.
2 Exodus International is an organisation linking together various local groups, in North America, that devote themselves to assisting homosexuals who want support in overcoming homosexuality.
3 Elizabeth R. Moberly, *Homosexuality: A New Christian Ethic* (Cambridge, U.K.: James Clarke, 1983). Moberly is both a theologian and a research psychologist with special interest in psychoanalytical research.
4 Leanne Payne, a former lecturer at Wheaton College, is a spiritually gifted woman with an internationally recognized ministry in the deliverance of homosexuals and other men and women with sexual problems. Her books include *The Broken Image* (Westchester, Ill.: Crossway, 1981) and *Crisis in Masculinity* (Westchester, Ill.: Crossway).
5 Lionel Ovessey, *Homosexuality and Pseudohomosexuality* (New York: Science House, 1969).
6 C.S. Lewis, *Mere Christianity*, p 89.

Chapter 8: Hidden Memories

1 In this case, oral incorporation of her father's phallus.
2 Payne's handling of the woman is a model of good spiritual
   care and is worth reading in its entirety. See Leanne
   Payne, *The Broken Image* (Eastbourne: Kingsway, 1988),
   pp. 15–27.
3 The details are enlarged in a paper by B. A. van der Kolk
   and Onno van der Hart, 'The Intrusive Past: The Flexibility
   of Memory and the Engraving of Trauma,' *American Imago*
   (John Hopkins University Press) 48, no. 4 (1991): 425–54.
   Much of what follows is taken from this excellent and
   detailed summary.
4 Ibid., p. 437.
5 Ibid., p. 429.
6 From unpublished lecture notes by John Smelzer, who can
   be contacted through Vineyard Ministries International,
   P.O. Box 65004, Anaheim, CA 92805. The lecture was
   given at a Vineyard conference. The questions that I am
   asking, though my own, were suggested to me as I listened
   to that lecture.
7 Ibid.

Chapter 9: Forgiving Family Sin

1 Francis Foulkes, *The Letter of Paul to the Ephesians*,
   Tyndale New Testament Commentaries (Leicester: Inter-
   Varsity Press 1989), p. 101.
2 Thomas Keating, *Open Mind, Open Heart* (Shaftesbury:
   Element, n.e. 1991), p. 9.
3 W. M. Thackeray, *Vanity Fair* (New York: Dutton/New
   American Library, 1962), chap. 35.
4 William Shakespeare, *Twelfth Night*, act 3, scene 4, line
   390.
5 See John White, *Excellent in Leadership* (Leicester: Inter-
   Varsity Press, 1986), chap. 1.
6 Ibid., pp. 22–24.

Chapter 10: Facing Your Repentant Future

1 Samuel W Gandy, 'I Hear the Accuser Roar,' in *Believers'
   Hymn Book* (London: Pickering and Inglis, n.d.), no. 93.

² *The Confessions of Saint Augustine*, trans. Rex Warner (New York: Mentor Books, 1963), pp. 182–83.

³ Charles W. Colson, *Against the Night* (Ann Abor, Mich.: Vine Books, 1989), p. 140.

⁴ John White, *Changing on the Inside* (Guildford: Eagle, 1991).

⁵ Charles G. Finney, *True and False Repentance* (Grand Rapids, Mich.: Kregel), pp. 14–15.

⁶ Charles W. Colson, *Born Again* (London: Hodder & Stoughton, 1979), pp. 116–17.

Chapter 11: Prayer: A Means of Grace

¹ Andrew Murray, *With Christ in the School of Prayer* (Alresford: CLC, 1983), p. 76.

² John Bunyan, *Grace Abounding* (Bletchley: Word, n.e.), pp. 45–46.

³ I have changed one or two of the facts in this account to protect the organisation concerned. The homosexuality was revealed and dealt with in private. But I note that in one or two New Testament occasions sin is dealt with publicly (Acts 5:1–10; 1 Cor 14:24–45).

⁴ Henri Nouwen, *The Way of the Heart* (London: Daybreak, 1990), p. 7.

⁵ Ibid., p. 8.

⁶ Thomas Keating is a former psychiatrist and author of a book about *centring* prayer, *Open Mind, Open Heart* (Shaftesbury: Element, n.e. 1991).

⁷ E. May Grimes, 'Speak, Lord, in the Stillness,' in *Hymns II* (Downers Grove, Ill.: InterVarsity Press, 1976), no. 140.

⁸ Nouwen, *The Way of the Heart*, pp. 31–32.

⁹ Thomas R. Kelly, *A Testament of Devotion* (New York: Harper & Row, 1941, n.e. 1992), p. 62.

Chapter 12: Healing Hidden Wounds Through the Body

¹ Such 'anointings' take various forms. People's subjective reactions to them vary, as does the language used to describe them in Scripture. I discuss the issue more fully in *When the Spirit Comes with Power* (London: Hodder & Stoughton, 1992).

² B. O. Banwell, 'Heart' in *New Bible Dictionary*, ed.

J. D. Douglas, 2nd ed. (Leicester.: InterVarsity Press, 1984), p. 465.
3 Leanne Payne, *Crisis in Masculinity* (Eastbourne: Kingsway, 1988), p. 35.

Chapter 13: The Healing Session

1 John Wimber with Kevin Springer, *Power Healing* (London: Hodder & Stoughton 1986), p. 199.
2 Ibid., p. 200.
3 Ibid., p. 207.
4 Ibid., pp. 207–10.
5 There is always a reason why this happens. Perhaps the commonest reason (not true in his case) is that of a return to a sin that gave rise to the condition in the first place, or of a refusal to repent in those cases where God has revealed the connection between a sin and the sickness. In most cases there is no connection between a specific sin and the sickness.

In this case, witchcraft and a powerful curse were involved. Later when we found out about the curse, partly through the Lord's revelations in the form of words and visions, and confirmed by the discovery of a cardboard box full of correspondence from the warlock who pronounced the curse, we sought to break its power. We thought we had triumphed, and we almost did. But always we had a nagging doubt, which in the long run proved to be true.

Nevertheless God's amazing purposes, both in the man's circle of friends, and in his denomination, were accomplished through the healing.

CHANGING ON THE INSIDE

The Keys to Spiritual Recovery

John White

* Can people really change?
* Do you long for change but doubt it can really happen?
* Are you afraid of the pain of changing?

Changing on the Inside will convince you that change for the better is not only possible, but essential. In this book Dr John White, a psychiatrist and author, draws on many years of experience to look closely at the relationship between repentance and emotional health. He examines the nature of healthy and lasting change – not superficial adjustments, not new resolutions, or outward conformity, but real change that results in peace, intimacy and a vital relationship with God.

John White is the author of *Eros Defiled, Excellence in Leadership, The Flight* and *When the Spirit Comes with Power*.

'I recommended *Changing on the Inside* to anyone who is seeking positive, permanent change from destructive behaviour patterns. John White says you can *change and he tells you how in a compelling and practical fashion.*'

John Wimber

'This book, better than any I know, gives us the anatomy of real repentance. Here we learn to see and repent of the depths of pride and sin revealed in our hearts, and we are remade.'

Leanne Payne

0 86347 044 0

EROS REDEEMED

Breaking the Stranglehold of Sexual Sin
John White

In Eros Redeemed the author expounds a biblical view of sexuality and offers extensive material on healing from sexual sin, addressing in greater detail and scope the topics discussed in *Set Free!*.

'Tens of thousands of Christians are in the grip of sexual sin,' claims John White. *'Not only are they looking for forgiveness, but are also looking for healing and a change that will make a permanent difference to their lives.'*

John White insists the stranglehold can be broken. Years of studying Scripture while ministering to those caught up in promiscuity, adultery, homosexuality, voyeurism and pornography have confirmed his belief. All can be redeemed from sexual sin.

In the face of radical feminism and gay liberation, the author lays the groundwork for change with a thoroughly biblical study of human sexuality and what it means to be a man or woman in Christ. He notes the consequences of sexual sin, the connection between promiscuity and violence, and the horrific effects of Satanic ritual abuse. He then offers the means of grace God has provided for inner healing and change.

'This is an important book for all in pastoral ministry of this kind to read. It may change your life: it will certainly enable you to be more confident and aware of God's grace and redeeming power in your ministry to others.'
Dr Gareth Tuckwell, *Renewal*

'This is a disturbing book in the best sense of the word. It helps us see ourselves naked and vulnerable before God, but being restored to the position we were created for in the Garden of Eden and will experience completely in Heaven.'
Mick Taylor, *Evangelism Today*

0 86347 112 9